Sunny Side Up

TO
virginia love &
with love,
best wishes. Thank
you for all you do
& all you are

Love,
Lucile (. . .

Sunny Side Up

Breakthrough ideas for women
from one of the most loved
speakers in the Church

LUCILE JOHNSON

COMPILED AND EDITED BY ARLENE BASCOM

Covenant
Communications, Inc.

Covenant Communications, Inc.
American Fork, Utah

Printed in the United States of America
First Printing: September 1993

Sunny Side Up
ISBN 1-55503-581-7
Library of Congress Catalog Card Number: 93-72257

Cover design by Roxanne R. Bergener
Photography by Ann Florence
Typographic design by Terry L. Jeffress

To my "Johnny"

*Who has always provided
my sunny days in the
gloomiest weather.*

❧ Contents ❧

❧Foreword❧

by H. O. Johnson

I've been married to Lucile for over fifty years. I know her pretty well. That's why Covenant asked me to introduce her to you. The story of how we met might give you an idea of her personality. Although Lucile had the classic female proportions during her college years which would have attracted any man to her, I can truthfully say I was attracted to her intellectually before I was ever aware of her physical appearance.

As a senior engineering student, I was enrolled in Psychology 1 as one of my electives. I sat on the front row in this classroom to seek some support from the teacher, because I had never seen so many girls, and they were overwhelming to me.

One day, the professor posed a question and looked around the room for a response, As we groped individually for our answers, the professor looked beyond me to someone in the back of the classroom, saying, "Miss Short, will you please give us your answer?" I listened in amazement to the answer Lucile gave, an explanation so meaningful and well-spoken I couldn't believe anyone could be that smart. Turning around, I got only a glimpse of a very pretty brunette with hair down past her shoulders.

When the class ended, I dashed out into the hall and positioned myself in a recess in the wall to see if I would recognize her as she came out of the classroom. I did, and I fell in behind her and began to ask myself what I should do next. We walked this way clear across the quadrangle to another building.

As she entered this building, I decided it was too late to do anything, but just then she turned around, curtsied slightly and said, "Well, how do I look from the front?" and that was the beginning of a relationship that has endured for more than fifty years.

Lucile grew up with a father who thought she could do no wrong. Lucile had great respect for her father and seldom challenged him. On one occasion however, she argued for a larger order at a restaurant and won. Just as he expected, she was not able to finish her meal, and the next morning when everyone else was served a delicious breakfast, she found only a leftover porkchop on her plate. So, even though Lucile was an only child for many years and somewhat spoiled, she did learn discipline.

She also learned self-confidence. Her confidence was evident at an early age. She was a born performer. For example, in the San Fernando valley where she was born, there was a talent show held each year. Many children were entered. The year Lucile was eight, the Short family attended the show. When the master of ceremonies asked, "Is there anyone else who would like to compete?" Lucile was on the stage before her parents could react. She requested the band play,"Yes Sir, That's My Baby" and she began to do the Charleston, and won the contest—much to the dismay of the other contestants who had been practicing for weeks.

People ask how Lucile got started as a lecturer in family affairs. She did not suddenly begin, but grew into the role over a period of many years. During our early married years, she was primarily a military wife, following her husband all over the world and raising our family of five children largely by herself, because I was gone to war much of the time. Lucile became a very capable and dependable mother, coping under trying circumstances, and always making the best of her situations. She belonged to, and worked with, wives' clubs and volunteer organizations wherever we were stationed and was involved with the Relief Society whenever it was available.

Lucile is a convert to the Church, and she gave many talks in church meetings over the years and proved herself to be an excellent teacher. At one time when she was teaching the Gospel Doctrine class she was told they had a more important assignment for her, and she was given a class of incorrigible teenagers who had run more than one teacher out. Over the weeks we saw a loving relationship develop between Lucile and every member of the class, and there was no more trouble with their discipline.

But, Lucile got her real start as a lecturer in Heidelberg, Germany, when we were stationed there. (It was about the time our own children were nearly all grown and gone.) She was asked to give the Christmas story at an Officers' wives Christmas luncheon. To pre-pare, Lucile read the entire book, *Jesus the Christ,* and spent many hours in prayer. At the conclusion of her talk, a line of tearful women came up to embrace her. The Commanding General's wife exclaimed, "My dear, I have just found the keynote speaker for the Protestant Women of the Chapel conference which is held each year in Berchtesgaden. There will be over five hundred women attending, and my husband will introduce you. Will you accept?"

She not only accepted but received a standing ovation at the end of that presentation, and after four more conferences, each one equal-ly successful, the Commander of US Army forces in Europe (called CINCEUR) created a new staff position for her, "Advisor to the CINC for Family Affairs." In addition to what the name implies, Lucile began counseling and lecturing troops and their dependents.

She is still well-known throughout the military community, because she understands the military and dependent military way of life as well as any woman living today. Because of this expertise and her long years of service, General Willard Pearson nominated her for the "Bob Hope Five Star Civilian Award for Service to Country," which was presented to her at Valley Forge in 1976.

Since returning to the United States, Lucile has addressed mili-tary families and service personnel throughout the country, as well as lecturing on the BYU Know Your Religion circuit for many years. She has also done a number of inspirational talk tapes which have been produced and distributed by Covenant Communications, Inc.

In 1987, Lucile and I fulfilled a special two-year assignment for The Church of Jesus Christ of Latter-day Saints as directors of the Visitors' Center at Hyde Park, in London, England. While there, Lucile was allowed to accept invitations to address various groups at military bases in England and Germany. She keynoted an army-wide conference for wives in October of 1988.

Another interesting sequel to her service with the military fami-lies is that when the United States forces began to mobilize for com-bat in the Middle East, Lucile was invited to address various troops and their families who were about to be separated. Almost no one has had more experience in going through this trauma than Lucile.

When she was a grandmother, Lucile returned to college, and she has never stopped learning. She has often said, "It is by pushing one's limits that life gets bigger and better."

Some women have asked her how she has done all this without neglecting her family, and she answers, "My family was essentially grown before all of this came about. Also, I was able to continue my education in absentia because the Army had contracts with various colleges and universities, and my husband gave me a great deal of encouragement and loving support every step of the way."

Lucile has been described in print as the most outstanding resource person in her field of sociology, with special expertise in marriage and family relations. She is presently a faculty member of the BYU Division of Continuing Education and travels extensively for the University throughout the United States and Canada. The Relief Society utilizes Lucile's talents as a speaker frequently and the invitations come from all over the United States, and she fulfills as many of them as possible. I believe she has amazing stamina, grace, and beauty for a woman in her seventies! Lucile followed me around the globe for thirty-five years, and now I am following her around the globe on her speaking assignments, as she continues to use her talents and knowledge to benefit others!

To conclude this introduction, I refer to a brief statement of our commitment to each other. When I entered the Army in 1939, a small booklet called, *The Officer's Guide,* stated that an officer is ever a gentleman, and his wife is his lady. I decided that from that moment on, I would treat my wife like the lady she is. I loved her, and there was something romantic about going through life married to a "lady." She has truly fulfilled my expectations, and I hope that I have always been her gentleman.

Acknowledgements

....

I am deeply indebted to Arlene Bascom, Darla Hanks Isackson, and all those at Covenant Communications who worked with skill, affection, and dedication to make this book possible.

I also wish to thank my five children: Colleen Kay Horne, Mark V. Johnson, Bart D Johnson, Patti Paula Lu Eddington, and Gary B. Johnson. Thank you for providing my wonderful memories involving each and every one of you. The book would not have been possible without you.

I am especially indebted to my husband for his support and patience in keeping me in one piece while the book was in process.

ᴖᴁ Introduction ᴁᴖ

Robert Louis Stevenson wrote a story of a ship caught in a raging storm. The passengers were terrified. They went below for safety as the boat pitched and tossed, but they were convinced they would all drown. The captain had lashed himself to the wheel to keep from being washed overboard. One desperate passenger crawled on his hands and knees to the pilot's station to talk to the captain. When he finally arrived, and looked up at the captain, the captain smiled at him. The passenger, no longer terrified, crawled back to the rest of the passengers shouting with joy, "We will not drown, we are going to be safe. The captain is smiling."

Why was the captain smiling? Perhaps it was false courage, but I don't think so. The captain had been in many storms before and had learned that a storm does not last forever, and would be followed by clear weather and sunshine.

So it is with our lives. Storms have their place, but they always pass. The buffeting of storms in our lives can bring about personal integrity if we weather the storm with courage and optimism. We could not easily develop courage and integrity if there were only blue skies and sunshine in our lives. But the secret of happy living in the midst of the storm is to hold fast to our belief that the sunshine will return. That makes the dark skies bearable.

I believe that life is a demanding school. We spend a brief time in this school. There are necessary lessons that only this earth school can teach. It is foolish to attend such a specialized university, to pay the high tuition that is required, and then skip out on the classes, burn the textbooks, or flunk the tests on purpose because we don't like the weather.

In my experience, life is not always "sunny-side-up", but if we approach the lessons that are in the storms, and the buffeting winds of adversity, with faith, and trust in the Lord's plan, we can always come through them "sunny-side-up." It is with this goal in mind that I share some of the lessons of life I have learned from those I have counseled with, from my family experiences, and from the scriptures. May these observations and my experiences, and the experiences of others which I share, be helpful in your journey through the storms of life.

Section One

Up with Marriage!

~≥ 1 ≤~
Warning Bells
and Success Strategies

....

A WARNING VOICE

On September 17, 1991, a power shortage at an AT&T switching center crashed the company computer system, leaving more than one million residents without phone service for more than seven hours. This power shortage also shut down all of New York's major airports, leaving thousands of passengers stranded in New York. As a result of the closed airports in New York, flights were also held up for tens of thousands of passengers across the country.

What was the catastrophe that caused this shortage? The next day, AT&T admitted that the men who manned the switching station had ignored both audio and visual alarms that signalled the computer system was losing power and was about to crash. When interviewed the men said, "We couldn't believe—just didn't believe—our eyes and ears. A crash just couldn't happen—certainly not with this computer system, which is one of the most sophisticated and reliable systems in the world!" Yet the crash did happen, and it could have been avoided if these men had listened to the warnings given them by the computer.

In the world, and in the Church, there are, at present, many flashing lights and warning bells going off to alert us that our marriages, families, testimonies, and relationships are in danger. You may think, "Not *my* marriage, not *my* children, and certainly not *my* testimony!" But I am raising a warning voice to tell you that no one is exempt from the dangers that surround us. Are you among those who ignore the warning signals and neglect making those greatly needed changes that will help you avoid a crash?

As Jesus ate the Passover meal with his apostles, he made a startling announcement: "Verily I say unto you, that one of you shall betray me" (Matt. 26:17). Judas knew to whom Jesus was referring, but the others began to look within their own hearts and asked with alarm: "Lord, is it I?" (v.18).

When small problems in our marriage, our relationships, and our attitudes start sending audio and visual warnings, too often we ignore them or deny them instead of asking "Is it I who needs to change?"

I have been a marriage therapist and family counselor for over twenty years. I feel strongly about the importance of family relationships. In fact, I feel all other priorities should be secondary to the success and the survival of our marriage and family relationships.

Through the years I have identified several essential elements that contribute to the success of a marriage. It almost goes without saying that love and acceptance combine to be number one in importance. Other vital factors include our personal spirituality, determination and will-ingness to work to make the marriage succeed, loyalty to each other, and willingness to forgive.

Isn't it time for each of us to do some personal introspection in each of these areas? If we are honest with ourselves and heed the promptings of the Spirit, we will recognize when it is time to move out of the "I-don't-have-a-problem" attitude into an attitude of "Lord-is-it-I?"

Prayerful introspection on a regular basis is absolutely necessary in today's temptation-laden society to keep from defaulting into serious trouble in our marriages.

Marriage is ordained of God. It is not a result of the laws of man, the state, the military, or the government. The principle of marriage pre-ceded all of these and was given to man by God. Matthew 19:5 states, "For this cause shall a man leave father and mother, and shall cleave to his wife: and they twain shall be one flesh."

The principles by which we become one with our spouses are the same principles by which we become one with God. Love is at the heart of our relationship with him, and love must be at the heart of our relationship with our spouse.

WE NEED TO FEEL WE ARE LOVED

I spoke to a military man who had recently battled cancer, and he said, "Lucile, I felt like I was betrayed by my own body." He had kept the word of wisdom. He prided himself upon his strong, healthy body.

Yet cancer zeroed in on him.

He said, "I felt that cancer had made me half a man. What good was I to my wife or to my children? I literally turned my head to the wall to die because I felt they would be better off without me."

The very day he made that decision, his wife came into his hospital room, shut the door, took off her coat, kicked off her shoes, and got up on the bed beside him. He said, "She put her sweet-smelling, fresh face close to mine. I can still remember the smell of her hair. As she spoke to me in soft tones about how much she loved me and how necessary it was for me to get well, I believe that moment was the catalyst that made a change in my body's defenses. What it was, I don't know, but something powerful took place, because after that day I could feel myself getting better.

"A nurse came in, looked at this situation with disapproval, and started to say something. My wife sat up and said, 'Don't you say a word. This is my husband, and we are going to lend comfort and solace to each other, and we're going to lick this thing.'"

That nurse smiled and bowed out, and they did lick that cancer.

Do you know what that husband needed to hear? He needed to hear that his wife really loved him. This man needed to know if he was worth saving and that he was that important to his wife. We all need to know we are important to someone. Does my husband love me? Does my mother love me? Does my father love me? Do the children love me? Does the Lord love me in spite of all my weaknesses? Am I really worthy of being loved? Most of the time we don't feel that we are, and we need constant reassurance.

When I am counseling, a husband might say, "Sister Johnson, this marriage is over. I've given it every shot." When he identifies the specific reasons he feels the marriage is over, I might say to him something like this: "I can't believe you are going to throw in the towel for such minuscule, incidental things. I want to know the bottom line." Generally, when we move through the mush, the bottom line is, "If she really loved me, she would do this or she wouldn't do that."

I hear exactly the same thing from wives. "I guess, Sister Johnson, if I really knew my husband loved me, I could accept this or that." That is what we all need, that assurance that we are loved.

Each of us have Love Banks with many different accounts in them—one for each person we know. People make their deposits and withdrawals from our Love Bank whenever we interact with them.

Happy, pleasurable interactions cause deposits to be made in the Love Bank, whereas painful interactions cause withdrawals. If there are not enough deposits in our Love Bank, we experience pain and sadness, which we often express in unkind or impatient actions toward others.

LOVE SUPPLIES

The human family has some universal emotional needs. The need to feel loved and accepted is chief among them. Most therapists have concluded that there are at least seven major categories they identify as *love supplies*, or ways we receive the love we are in need of. I will address only the top three—identified as the favorite love supplies. They are (1) the need to be listened to with empathy and understanding, (2) the need for verbal affection, which means having someone show affection through words, and (3) the need for physical affection.

What do these love supplies do for a person? They cause us to feel better about ourselves, to have clearer vision about our lives. These love supplies heal, soothe and even render peace of mind to the receivers.

Can you name your own favorite love supplies? What are your spouse's favorites? Thousands of people identified as number one the importance of *being listened to*. They wanted to be listened to with empathy, with understanding. We call this *active* listening.

These people are saying to their loved ones, "Don't tune me out. Don't dismiss what I am saying by acting bored or indifferent. Make an *effort* to hear and understand what I am saying."

The love supply that was listed as second in importance was *verbal affection*. Verbal affection means showing affection through words— words that encourage, lift, or praise. Mark Twain said, "I could live for two months on one good compliment." Haven't we all felt an immediate boost from some admiring word that came our way and then recalled it again and again?

This summer my husband and I were on a trip to Yellowstone Park and Jackson Hole, Wyoming. We stayed one night in a joint family vacation home in Ashton. When I don't have a definite deadline to meet, such as a plane to catch, I am inclined to dawdle and drag my feet. I knew Johnny was anxious to get out on the road, but I was slow getting lunch made and myself ready. I saw him sitting quietly in a chair, dressed, packed, and ready to go, but he didn't display one bit of impatience or irritability. I said, "Johnny, I want you to know how much I appreciate how sweet and patient you are when I am such a slowpoke this morning and I want to thank you."

He said, "Isn't that interesting? I was just thinking how much I appreciate all *you* do. It was a great breakfast, and you did all of the cleaning on this place so we can leave it spic and span for the rest of the family who come here. Now you are making us a great lunch we will enjoy while looking over Yellowstone Falls, and I want to thank *you*."

That is verbal affection.

The third favorite love supply is *physical affection*—not merely sexual, but all expressions of tenderness and affection that reach out to lift. The tender touch and the hug that has no hidden agenda are both examples of physical affection that can be offered with no strings attached.

There's a strong connection between the sexual satisfaction of a woman and the amount of non-sexual touching the husband gives her outside the bedroom. Intimate love in marriage is greatly enhanced by physical touching that has nothing to do with sexual activity.

THE LOVE PRINCIPLE IN MARRIAGE

The *Love Principle* is very important in marriage. The *Love Principle* states that when one person is loving, others tend to act in the same loving way. A quote from Orson Pratt, who has been one of my favorite writers since I first joined the Church, explains what I mean by this principle. Elder Pratt said,

> The more righteous the people become, the more they are qualified for loving others and rendering them happy. A wicked man can have but little love for his wife. While a righteous man, being filled with the love of God, is sure to manifest this heavenly attribute in every thought and feeling of his heart, and in every word and deed. Love and joy and innocence will radiate from his very countenance and be expressed in his every look. And this will beget confidence in the wife of his bosom. And she will love him in return. For love begets love, and happiness imparts happiness. And these heaven-born emotions will continue to increase more and more until they are perfected and glorified in all the fullness of the eternal love itself.

We truly experience in our lives what we give. In other words, if we give love, we get it back, but if we are feeling unloved, we may act in unloving ways, and will therefore not receive the love we need—only more of the same unloving actions that we are giving out. It is something of a vicious cycle, but if we understand the dynamics, we can break the cycle by giving out more of what we need, even if we don't feel like doing it.

This principle works in the simplest acts of life, something as fleeting as a smile. If we give a smile, our partners return the smile. If we raise our voice and argue, our partners will follow suit. But, when we calm down and speak softly, our mates usually will too.

The implication in our marriages is this: If my marriage is in a non-loving mode, I need to ask, "Lord, is it I? Am I being self-centered? Is it I who is being selfish and unloving, or am I showing concern about my mate's happiness and well-being?"

Paul and Moroni each gave us some excellent reasons why the quality of love is vital in our marriages. Paul said,

> Though I speak with the tongue of men and of angels, and have not charity, I am become as sounding brass, or a tinkling cymbal. And though I have the gift of prophecy, and understand all mysteries, and all knowledge; and though I have faith, so that I could move mountains and have not charity I am nothing. (1 Cor. 13:1–2)

Moroni adds,

> Wherefore, cleave unto charity, which is the greatest of all, for all things must fail—But charity is the pure love of Christ, and it endureth forever; and whoso is found possessed of it at the last day, it shall be well with him. (Moro. 7:46–47)

A woman once came to London to tell me about her husband. Her patriarchal blessing counseled her to fast for two days whenever she had an important problem she needed to solve, then to take it to the Lord, which is exactly what she had done. She said, "I received my answer, and I was absolutely stunned. Because after I told Heavenly Father what Bill had done and what he hadn't done, and that I was broken-hearted, the only words I heard were 'I love Bill.'"

The woman continued, "I could not believe I would get that reply from my petition. After all the things that Bill had done, how could the Lord love Bill?" The answer, of course, is that Heavenly Father does not love us because of what we do or do not do, but because we are his children. Obviously the Lord knew something about Bill that this wife didn't know about him. Jesus and our Heavenly Father love all of us unconditionally, and they know our divine potential.

With this new information, it became her responsibility to look at Bill as the Lord looks at him, with divine potential, a great lesson for us all. If we will ask the Lord to help us love our husbands or wives the way he loves them, we will be able to see them in a new way.

Christlike love is kind, but our ability to be kind is not automatic; it takes practice. Christlike love is patient, but our ability to be patient does not come about like turning a light switch on and off. Christlike love is total acceptance of others where they are right now, an unconditional love that must be learned. Since Christlike love is the one thing absolutely necessary for a celestial marriage, we must be willing to work at developing these qualities.

Good works, paying our tithing, good income, rearing children properly, having a clean, peaceful home—these are all good but they are not the bottom line. They will all profit us nothing *unless* we have charity, or this Christlike love. Then when we have developed charity, the other things simply add to the quality of our marriages.

If we don't have Christlike love we cannot have a truly successful marriage. We can have a mediocre marriage, but *we cannot have a fully successful marriage in the eyes of our Heavenly Father without Christlike love, just as we cannot have a successful life in the eyes of our Heavenly Father without Christlike love.*

Last year, after a massive heart attack and a quadruple bypass, my husband was in an Intensive Care Unit. Our five children and I stood around his bed as he was fighting for his life. It was a very sober time for us. He lay there with tubes down his throat and a clamp in his mouth. His eyes were closed and the machine was breathing for him. Even though he seemed unconscious, each of the children expressed their love for their father—and told him why he had to live. The youngest, a son, said, "Dad, you have to live for *me*. The other kids have had you longer than I have—Colleen has had you 20 years longer than I have."

Our youngest daughter said, "Dad, you have to live for me and for my children who have no father. You are the only father figure they have."

When each had spoken and many tears had been shed, I said, "You are *all wrong*, he must live for *me*."

My son said, "Mother, you've had him longer than any of us.

You've had him for fifty-two years!"

I replied, "Yes, but I want him for fifty-two zillion years!"

We did not know whether he heard us, but when the tubes and clamp were finally out, he told us his feelings as he had listened to each of us in a way he had never heard before. He told us how desperately he had wanted to speak. Now my husband has always been the silent type, by choice. He is a great mathematician and scientist, but a great conversationalist he is not. But in this painful, frightening situation, he realized that he yearned to speak of love.

He said, "I wanted to tell each of you children of my appreciation and love. But most of all, I wanted to tell your mother how much I love her! My feelings were so intense that from the top of my head to the bottom of my feet I was filled with an awesome love. What if I could never again speak to tell her this? I couldn't bear to think of the pain it would cause me."

WHAT DOES A GOOD MARRIAGE REQUIRE OF US?

When my husband and I had our forty-fifth anniversary, we thought it would be a very good time for us to sit down and make a marriage journal for our posterity. We wanted our progeny to know the things through which we had walked in these long years and to know that marriage doesn't automatically ensure happiness forever after. We wanted our children and their children to know that a good marriage requires effort and implies growth.

My husband said, "Lucile, I want our posterity to know that in marriage, no matter what happens, you never give up." Then he described to me an address he had heard Winston Churchill, the great British statesman, give. Standing among his officers, he had said to them, "Never give up, never, never, never give up." With that he sat down, having given one of the shortest addresses anybody had ever heard. But it was a powerful one, and the officers who heard him never forgot it.

My husband and I also wanted our posterity to understand the importance of unconditional love. We both believe that unconditional love means wanting to share with someone everything that is good, happy, and positive in this life. It means you do not have to earn my love, and I do not have to earn yours; that is conditional love. Unconditional love means that of my own volition, with my free agency, I have chosen you, from all whom I might have chosen, to be my eternal companion, to share both my joy and my grief, as you have chosen to share them with me.

Unconditional love means we accept each other. We accept each other with all our failures, faults, idiosyncrasies, and weaknesses.

For many people, courtship is fairly unrealistic. In the courtship period it is "moon and June and spoon" and all those delicious things, and we have blinders—romantic blinders—on our eyes. People in love view the person they are courting as absolutely perfect. If in the engagement period you find a few little tacky things you don't like, you're sure you will be able take care of that after the marriage. They'll change. Then when you say "I do" and begin the process of redoing, you discover that your beloved resists your attempts to "re-do" them.

It is at this point that we learn that accepting our companion as they are is the only way to allow them to grow and change. Our acceptance allows them the freedom to change. It is through the *acceptance process* that we each grow.

Part of acceptance is accepting that we are going to encounter problems, and it is our great growth-producing opportunity as we move through marriage to solve the problems that inevitably will come. How could we expect it to be otherwise in the intimate and fragile environment of marriage? Two human beings together under these circumstances will naturally have abrasive situations at times.

Why should we demand perfection in our wife or in our husband? What is perfect? Perfect means complete, finished, fully developed. Your husband or your wife is not complete, nor is your relationship or life itself. We are each in the process of becoming. Therefore, how can we expect perfection in each other?

People often come to me with that lament: they have discovered imperfections in their spouse, and as a result, they are disillusioned. People who continue to try marriage a second and a third time often believe that "somewhere out there" they are going to find that perfect person. I have news for them. Their search will be in vain, because there *is* no such perfect person.

Let's say there *was* one perfect person and you found her or him. But you yourself are not perfect, so you would blow the whole relationship—a perfect person might not want you and so you are right back at square one where you were before!

Elder Neal Maxwell once gave a provocative address that asked the question, "Why do we demand perfection in our relationships?" He used an interesting analogy to put his point across. He described a home in the process of being constructed. There is scaffolding and open buckets of paint and clutter all around. He asked, "Do we make any value judgments on that? No. We're willing to reserve judgment until the house is finished. Why can't we be at least this understanding in our relationships one with another?"

The important point to remember is that our own growth can come about *because* of the imperfection in others. Your companion's faults and failings can offer you a tremendous opportunity for your own growth.

A woman who had waited quite a long while to find the proper man to marry came to counsel with me. She felt she had been betrayed in her marriage. She said, "I wanted a man who was a spiritual giant. I wanted one knowledgeable in the scriptures who would have the spiritual dynamics to lead out in the home, because that's my failing. I needed that in a companion. I thought I found him, but after I married him I discovered he wasn't a spiritual giant at all, and I am so disillusioned. I feel I've been betrayed . . . I don't think I can stay in this marriage. You've got to help me."

I asked, "What have you done as a result of this discovery?"

When I could lead her a little further into what I meant, she said, "I can tell you one thing, I have never read the scriptures so much in my life."

"What else?" I asked.

"I'm on my knees praying constantly," she replied. "I didn't know I had the stamina to be on my knees as much as I'm required to be. I have to have help, and I've discovered that is the only place I get it."

I said, "What other terrible things have you been required to do since you've discovered this flaw in your husband?"

She started to smile when she recognized the direction I was taking. I told her I was not being lightminded when I asked the question, "Has it ever occurred to you that how we react to the imperfection in others determines our own growth? As we learn to react appropriately, we grow. This is not necessarily the case for the other person, but we grow."

We might even thank Heavenly Father for the imperfections we see in our companion, because these imperfections may allow us to grow in ways we might not otherwise have grown.

Most marriages begin with love, but they can't proceed successfully without the discipline of focusing on positive ways to nourish, express, and enhance that love.

Loving someone else unconditionally takes character, and character is not automatic. Character develops as we resolve to pay the price. Character requires that we do not put ourselves in a position of cement. Marriage also requires this flexibility. Sometimes we take a stand we think is good and proper and irrevocable, and we will not move from that position even when our spouse gives us very good reasons for moving. Unconditional love, on the other hand would be evidenced in flexibility and willingness to bend and change for the good of both parties in the marriage.

SPIRITUALITY IN MARRIAGE

Whatever a couple's spiritual and religious persuasion might be, I feel that a marriage cannot ever be really called a marriage unless it has spirituality as its keystone. The dictionary definition of keystone is the stone piece at the crown of an arch that locks the other pieces in place. I believe that is what spirituality is to a marriage.

I am a product of the Church, and I consider the Church to be the greatest spiritual educational institution in the world, barring none. The Book of Mormon has been a witness to me that Jesus is the Christ. Studying this great book can bring you to a greater depth of understanding of the cornerstone of our religion, who is the Lord Jesus Christ—but reading and studying the Book of Mormon *together* will bring you closer to each other as husbands and wives. It can be the greatest marriage manual you will ever read.

President Ezra Taft Benson has said that the Book of Mormon is a schoolmaster that will bring us to Christ. There is a difference between those who *read* the Book of Mormon and those who *know* the Book of Mormon. Our prophet has promised us that if we will read it, so that we know it, the Book of Mormon will bring discernment, insight, conviction and peace into our lives. Can you see how these qualities will enrich your marriage and help you succeed in making your marriage the kind of a marriage Heavenly Father wants you to have?

On a recent tour, I asked a young woman in Atlanta, Georgia, to meet me at the airport because she had a story she wanted to share with me. She said she and her husband were not happy in their marriage, and as a matter of fact she was very disillusioned because of the ugly words that were increasing in their relationship. She went to her bishop, and asked him, "What can I do? I don't believe I can stay in this marriage unless he changes." She said, "The bishop gave me this advice, 'I recommend that you get up at least an hour earlier than your husband and your children every morning. Set the alarm to make sure you'll do this, then in the quiet sanctity of your living room, you read for one full hour in the scriptures.'"

This young woman said to me, "The bishop promised me there would be some wonderful differences in my marriage, and I thought all the change would be in my husband. I felt something wonderfully, remarkably, dynamic would take place in him. But," she continued, "my husband didn't change a whit even though I faithfully followed my bishop's advice.

"But something happened to *me!* I began to find the great power of reading for an hour in the scriptures before I would begin my day. It was like the armor of God in my life. It was like his arms were around me. I could hear my husband say things that previously would devastate me and invite an angry retort. But I found it wasn't necessary to respond in kind. I could look at him with love and understanding, realizing he really didn't know what he was saying." That is the power of the scriptures in our lives.

As a counselor, I always turn my clients, whatever their religious persuasion might be, to the scriptures. Then I have the temerity to suggest to them, not that their partner might dramatically change, but that I can promise them unequivocally that some wonderful things will happen for—or to—*them.*

People sometimes go out of their way to justify their behavior. A woman came to me, and said, "Lucile, you always turn to the scriptures as a therapist, and you talk about Ephesians and Corinthians as being marriage manuals. What if I could prove to you from the scriptures that I have a justification for leaving my husband?"

I said, "I'd be delighted to hear it."

She quoted me Ephesians 4:22, "Put off . . . the old man [whose ways are] corrupt." I assured her that the way she was interpreting that scripture wasn't quite what the Lord had in mind!

In May 1990, my husband and I were in Germany. I was invited to address the military forces from one end of Germany to the other, and we concluded in East Berlin. It was an awesome experience for us. I met a young couple there, and the wife told me their story. She had joined the Church six years before coming to Germany, but her husband had not. He was a distinguished graduate of Princeton University and had several advanced degrees and prided himself, as she said, upon his intellectual accomplishments and his abilities.

When this young wife was converted to the Church, she said, "My husband acted only vaguely amused, and our otherwise good marriage began to deteriorate because of his superior attitude. The marriage became so bad I realized it couldn't continue as it was going. The Church meant so much to me, and for the first time I was facing in the proper direction in my life. I concluded there were only two things that could happen to get me out of the conflict in my situation. Either my husband had to die (which wasn't the happiest thought), or I would have to divorce him. I saw no other way.

"My bishop pointed out that there *was* another solution. He asked me, 'What would happen if your husband was converted?' I countered with 'That's impossible. My husband has such intellectual pride he will never be able to be in tune sufficiently to accept the truth of the gospel.'"

But the bishop asked her, "Is anything too hard for the Lord?" He also reminded her to consider the power of fasting and prayer.

She said, "Sister Johnson, that's exactly what I did. I asked Heavenly Father to send two missionaries—missionaries who were brilliant, well-educated, and sophisticated. I wanted him to send two missionaries who had great self-assurance, because they would need those qualities to get through to my husband.

"Then one night someone knocked at our door and my husband answered it. Guess who was standing there? Two senior missionaries, a husband and wife. They were elderly, Sister Johnson, as old as you are. They were frail, and they came from a farm; they were obviously ill at ease. I thought, 'Oh no. Why would Heavenly Father do this?' I felt he couldn't have sent two missionaries more inappropriate than these two. Didn't he hear my prayer? But do you know what? My husband invited them in and they stayed for an hour and a half, and then he invited them back the next week, and the next. And Sister Johnson, at the end of six weeks that farmer with less than perfect hearing and grammar took my husband down into the waters of baptism."

Heavenly Father knew that this sophisticated, rather arrogant, prideful "PhDer" needed that set of humble and precious missionaries and this couple needed that experience. It was a very good experience for this elderly couple, who sacrificed a lot to go on that mission, leaving their home, their children and grandchildren so this young man could hear the gospel.

I know Heavenly Father answers prayers, maybe not instantaneously but I know they are answered in our Father's way and in his time. From my long years of experience with prayers having been answered, and some delayed before they were answered, I have an absolute conviction that Father is always on time.

I used to believe that prayer was rather a simplistic thing, but let me share with you what I have learned from Brigham Young. He said that prayer is often difficult and it's strenuous. It's just plain hard work. And if you really want to converse with the Lord, you must count on a mighty struggle. Receiving inspiration and revelation through prayer is one of the greatest achievements of man, and to expect that blessing without effort is contrary to the order of heaven.

We have to break the prayer barrier by knocking and knocking. We should not be dismayed when after much knocking, it seems to avail little. There are few exercises of faith greater than that of praying persistently. If you want changes in your relationship or in your own life, then be prepared to plead and pray for the presence of the Holy Ghost in your life and in your marriage. Your marriage will have a depth in its dimension in direct relationship to these spiritual qualities.

"Call home" often as you work to make your marriage succeed. God knows exactly where you are and he hears your prayers and understands your tears. I plead for us as couples to stand together in holy places and sustain and love each other in what must be very tremulous times that lie ahead.

The priesthood class in my ward was discussing the Holy Ghost and how they could recognize the presence of the Holy Ghost striving with them. A friend shared with me what my husband told this class. He said, "Your husband stood—this great patriarch—and he said to us 'Have you ever entered your home quietly so your wife didn't know you were standing at the kitchen door? Maybe she was at the stove or at the sink doing something very simple, and as you watch her, such an overwhelming feeling of love and respect for her just washes over you, and before you know it, there are tears in your eyes? Maybe you're not accustomed to tears in your eyes. What do you do with those feelings? Too often as men we just brush them away with some embarrassment and move into the family room, perhaps, to read the paper." But he continued, "Don't do that. Because when that feeling overwhelms you, this is a manifestation of the Holy Spirit prompting you. If you act upon those feelings, you will become more conversant with them so you will understand them and recognize them when they come. Go to that wife of yours, put your arms around her, tell her what you are feeling and how much you love her, and that will increase those tender feelings in your marriage."

Would there be anything more important for which we should pray than to have the constant presence of that great Spirit personage in our lives to help us be the kind of a marriage partner we should be? That should be a keystone in your marriage.

In Hawaii this past year a Know Your Religion speaker from BYU became ill and could not fill his assignment. He asked his wife if she could give his presentation. She told him she couldn't do that but she could give her own presentation, and she was very good.

She related from her own experience a stressful period of time in her marriage. The couple had six children, and she was pregnant with the seventh. She shared how overwhelmed she felt. She was never able to get through the relentless daily demands, and she felt as though she were drowning.

Speaking to friends and family she asked, "What can I do to fill my own needs?" Several advised her to go back to school and take an art or music course, anything she felt would be just for her.

Then she took her discouragement to the Lord. The spiritual impression she received was to LOVE HER HUSBAND. She was impatient with that input. "I *do* love my husband," she thought. But each time she wearied the Lord, the impression was the same, LOVE YOUR HUSBAND. "How can that help fill *my* needs?" she wondered. But she began to think of those things she knew her husband liked. She decided to show him how much she loved him. Her husband had a demanding job, they had little money and a big family. She didn't have time or money to do big things. However, she made a list of the little things she knew made him happy. Each day she made sure one of the things on that list was done.

One morning he was rushing to leave for the campus, and she realized he didn't have a clean white shirt. This was important to him, so she began digging into the ironing basket for a shirt to iron. (She confessed she was about two years behind in her ironing!)

As she was getting the shirt, her husband shouted from upstairs, "Come up to the bathroom so we can talk while I shave."

She shouted back, "I can't, I'm going to iron a shirt for you." In a moment, she heard a kerplunk-kerplunk. It was her husband dragging the ironing board upstairs so they could talk for a few minutes while she ironed his shirt. She was touched.

What did they talk about? He wanted her to know how much he loved and appreciated her and all the things she did for him to make him happy. He said he didn't think he could manage the stress and overload of his job if it weren't for her. "You make all the difference," he told her.

What had happened to this husband? This kind of verbal affection had not been a natural part of his personality. Later, this wife learned that he had become increasingly concerned about how tired and discouraged she seemed. In his prayers he had asked his Heavenly Father what he could do to help her. The prompting he received was similar to the prompting she had received, "Let her know you love her." He was impatient with his answer, just as the wife had been with hers. "She knows I love her," he responded. But when that same prompting was repeated, he decided that the Lord knew he loved her, and he knew he loved her, but maybe she didn't know it. So, in his own way he began to plan simple and small ways to tell her and show her how much he loved her. The promptings of the Holy Ghost had helped each partner be more sensitive to the needs of the other.

GROWTH-GIVING FORGIVENESS

The Lord tells us in Matthew 6:14–15 if you will forgive men their transgressions, your Father will also forgive you. But, if you do not forgive men, your Father will not forgive you your transgressions.

Can Father, or *will* Father, answer our prayers if he *cannot* forgive us because we have not forgiven others? Are your prayers, perhaps, not answered as fully or swiftly as you would wish? Have you ever considered that you may have IOU's you need to tear up—IOU's against your husband or others who have hurt you or transgressed against you in some way, maybe even years ago?

Jesus said that whenever you stand to pray, forgive. If you have anything against anyone, he says, forgive, so that your Father who is in heaven can forgive you. Marriage gives us almost daily opportunities to learn how to forgive.

I counseled a wife who had some serious problems in her marriage because her husband did not understand her. They had several young children, and he worked more than one job as he continued his education at BYU, and she had a job in her home, as well, taking telephone calls to bring in a little extra money. When this husband came home, he was extremely critical of her and how he found the house, never taking into account that she was caring for so many little children in addition to working at the telephone job. One day she said to me, "I can no longer live in this marriage because my husband gives me no understanding or support. All I hear from him is criticism."

But then something happened. She confided that one night her husband helped her bathe the children and put them in bed, and, in this rather run-down house where they lived, with an old-fashioned bathtub on legs, something remarkable happened. It did not happen in a chapel, nor in the temple, but in a bathroom that wasn't very clean after bathing several children. She said, "After we put the children to bed, I said to my husband, 'We need to talk.' We went into this old-fashioned bathroom, shut the door, and he sat on the edge of the bathtub and I on the commode. I had a list of my grievances. I said, 'I want you to know that I am not going to be able to stay with you. I cannot forgive your cruelty and your unkindness.'"

She went down through her list of the wrongs she felt he had committed. Then she said, "I looked at my husband, and I could tell the emotion he was feeling by the knots in his jaw, and his white knuckles, but he never said a word.

"Then, in that least likely place, as I was going through my recitation of grievances, there came a spirit personage—we know not who—but we felt of the glory and peace that he brought. We could not see visually who he was, but I knew my husband felt his presence, too, because he looked at me with a startled look on his face. We barely breathed, but I was the one who received the information from that spirit personage. These were the words I heard, 'You must forgive your husband. You must forgive him every day of every week of every month, if it is necessary. You must forgive him. Not because he deserves it, but you must, because if you do not, you will halt your eternal progression.'"

In the fragile and intimate setting of marriage, we are given ample opportunity to practice forgiving because hurts are sure to come. We can not only learn to forgive others, but to become humble enough to ask for forgiveness.

If you want to learn to love your spouse unconditionally, ask him or her to forgive you, even if you are the one smarting. It is remarkable how asking for forgiveness can soften hearts. It may be helpful to ask your partner on a regular basis, "Have I done anything this week to hurt your feelings or make you sad or angry? If I have, please forgive me."

In 3 Nephi 12:23–24 we read,

Therefore, if ye shall come unto me, or shall desire to come unto me, and rememberest that thy brother [or husband] hath aught against thee—Go thy way unto thy brother, and first be reconciled to thy brother, and then come unto me with full purpose of heart, and I will receive you.

This scripture tells us that it requires more than just an "effort" toward reconciliation. A full reconciliation must actually take place, which means you are required to do whatever is necessary to bring about that reconciliation.

LOYALTY IN MARRIAGE

I cannot think of any quality that is more endearing, more enduring, or more needful in a marriage than loyalty. Have you been uncomfortable at parties, or at a restaurant, when a husband and a wife, smiling rather tightly at each other, take little bites out of one another? We know our companion's failures. We know their weak points. We know where they are most vulnerable. It is absolutely the epitome of disloyalty to be out in public and make those things known.

Be loyal to one another. If your companion is doing something out in public, whether it's the way he is eating his soup or the way she is behaving, you would be wise not to bring that to his or her attention in front of anybody.

If a behavior bothers you, wait until you get home, but it is not wise to advise your companion of your irritation over that behavior in front of the children either! Be totally, absolutely loyal and point out these things you wish could be changed in the privacy of your bedroom.

I consider it the height of disloyalty for one parent to point out another parent's failures or insufficiencies in front of the children. Sometimes a parent will do this hoping, perhaps, to seek the child's support for his or her position. Don't place your children in a position where they have to "take sides" or hear unkind or demeaning or negating things about a parent. As a matter of fact, be the *most* loving and supportive in front of your children. Also, be loyal about your companion to your parents and to his or her parents. Say only those things that are loving and supportive about each other.

I'd like to share with you a little experience I had with a young girl who came back from her honeymoon alone, ran into her parent's home, and into her bedroom, and slammed the door. Her parents could not achieve any communication with her as she sobbed in her bedroom. They did, however, secure permission to call me, and she agreed to talk with me.

Can you imagine the things that went through my mind as I waited for this young woman's arrival? I knew this young girl, I knew her husband, and it was a temple marriage. What were the things he had demanded on the honeymoon that were so offensive to her that she had to leave a bridegroom and return to her own home alone?

I went through all these things in my mind, and when she finally arrived with tear-stained face, I placed this pretty little girl in front of me and tried to encourage her gently to reveal the awful things which might have been the reason for her distress. As I made illusion to the kinds of things I was thinking of, she was horrified. "No, no," she said.

Finally, she shared with me what had happened. They had gone to an area where they had found other young people whom they had known at the university also celebrating their honeymoons. One night they all decided to get together for dinner, and it was a fun evening. Then they began to tell funny little things that had happened to each of them, and they were laughing. In this intimate environment, some of the things that began to be shared were not quite so funny.

Her husband had made the observation "We have been told what little girls are made of. They're made of sugar and spice and everything nice but I know now what little girls are really made of. They are made of powder and paint and things that *ain't*." The fellows, picking up on that, began to laugh.

What this young bridegroom went on to imply was that his wife's bust size was a bit of a surprise. That was unkind and disloyal in the extreme. Not a single woman at that table even smiled, but the men thought it was hilariously funny.

This young bride excused herself from the table, went back to the room, packed her suitcase, took the keys to the car and drove home. Her husband searched for her in agony and terror, and finally found her. Later, I talked to him about loyalty. If he had any feelings of having been "deceived" as far as his little wife's bust size was concerned, if he had been as loyal as he should have been, he could have shared with her these things privately.

Of course, it would be the kind thing perhaps for him to say, "I think you have a beautiful body, but if you want to wear a padded bra, if it's important to you, that's fine with me, but I want you to know, I think you're absolutely beautiful just the way you are."

I asked that young husband, "Are these words you could honestly say?"

He said, "Oh yes, absolutely!" But that was *not* the message she had received at all.

Let's be loyal to each other . . . to be so honorably loyal to each other that we will never allow anyone—not a child or a mother or a mother-in-law—to come between the two of us; nor ever, ever be caught bad-mouthing each other. As husbands and wives we know each other well enough that it may be a temptation to show up the weaknesses that we know exist in our companion, especially those that cause us some discomfort. If we are ever to be as "one" as the Lord wants us to be, it is illogical for us to be critical of the other half of ourselves.

Unconditional love demands that we be praising toward our partners, and let our children know we will never display any disloyalty at all toward their mother or father. We need to stand together in our loyalty. Children are masters at pitting one parent against the other. They learn how to do that very early, and I've seen marriages where, as a matter of fact, children will align with one parent against another. Don't allow that!

The very best thing a father can do for his children, far more important than buying them things, is to love their mother and to compliment her and hold her up as a shining example. She will strive to rise to fulfill that loving prophecy placed on her.

Likewise, the best thing mothers can do for their children is to love their fathers and to let them know what a great father they have and point out the noble qualities she sees in him.

You might think the size of your home or how many Persian rugs are on the floor will be important in your children's memories. They will not. Mothers sometimes think that a pristinely clean house and clean clothes and meals will be the things their children will remember. It is not so. What your children will recall, as they grow up and leave the home and have families of their own, will be the *feelings* that were in your home. If they are fortunate, they will remember the feelings of love and loyalty that existed between their mother and their father.

I was in Idaho for a university program, and one night the husband and wife who brought me back to my motel had one of their sons sitting in the back seat with his wife and little baby. As they drove up to the motel this man said to me. "I have a son here sitting beside you, and the story I want to tell you concerns him."

This fine family were dairy farm people, they had seven sons, no daughters. I met some of those sons—great big strapping boys, and their father was a great big man. He said, "I learned early as these boys came along that it was necessary for me as the father and the disciplinarian to stand between them and their mother. I let them know I would abide no insubordination or rudeness to her. I thought I did a pretty good job, but one night I came in earlier than usual from the dairy herd and I heard the voice of this boy and the tearful words of my wife.

"As the argument got more heated, I couldn't believe the things this boy said, and I was so angry that he would speak in this disrespectful manner to his mother. I stood outside the door to wait till the very last word was uttered."

When this fifteen-year-old stomped out of that bedroom, he slammed smack into his six-foot-two, two-hundred pound father. He was a bit taken aback and said, "Ohhh, Da-Dad? I didn't know you were there."

His dad said, "Obviously you didn't." He continued, "I felt the time for words had passed and the time for action had arrived. I gently folded up my fist and let him have one little cuff on the side of the jaw. Totally taken by surprise, he lost his balance and landed on the floor. I went and stood over him."

Can't you visualize this? This colossus standing over this kid? Then this father said in no uncertain terms to that teenager, "Don't let me ever hear you speak in a manner like that to your mother again. I will never, ever allow such ugliness toward your mother. She is my wife and my eternal companion."

I said, "Brad, is this the way you remember the incident?"
He said, "Yes."
I said, "Would you mind sharing your feelings about what happened?"
He said, "Well, my first feeling was that I thought my dad had cracked my jaw. And I was angry and humiliated and all of those feelings that anybody would have, but, I'm glad you asked me that question because strangely enough I felt happy. I had a feeling of pride. All I could think was 'Wow! My dad really loves my mother!' Maybe I'd never realized that before. As a fifteen-year-old, I made a decision about the kind of a woman I would seek and marry in the proper place, and we would be as loyal to each other as my mom and dad."

When we think of loyalty, we might think of husband and wife standing together, backing each other up. One husband told me "My wife is a nag, and she is too fat." He was no tall, slim, reed himself. Then he went on to say, "The house is always a mess, there's no order or system at all." These things had some viability, I'm sure, but evidently he made them known to the butcher, the baker, and the candlestick maker. *Everybody* heard these complaints.

When I asked his wife to explain how she saw the marriage, she said to me, "The thing that hurts me the worst is his criticism about my weight. I know I have gotten too heavy. I went on a diet without telling him, and I lost twenty pounds. One night when I said to him, 'Do you know I've been on a diet?'

"He said, 'Oh, you have?'

"I told him I had lost twenty pounds.

"He looked up from the paper briefly and said, 'Good, now lose a hundred more!'"

How poor that timing was and how disloyal! If he could have expressed appreciation for what she had already done, can you see the different effect it would have had? Her next remarks were not surprising to me. "You see, he doesn't even notice or care. It's the same way about the house. Whenever I really try to keep this house clean, he comes in and never makes one single observation about it, and so I think, 'What's the use? It doesn't really matter.'"

I turned to this husband and asked, "Don't you notice when the house is clean?"

"Well, yeah, I do," he said.

I asked, "Why don't you say something?"

He replied, "I don't really think about it."

Do you know that most of the time when our partners seem cruel, it isn't premeditated; it is just careless. The things that hurt us, many of the things that are inappropriate as far as timing is concerned, or as far as loyalty is concerned, are simply the result of carelessness or thoughtlessness.

This wife shared another thing that was the most difficult of all. She said her five children have had a lot of respiratory problems, so she has had to take the children to the doctor many times. She can't afford to have a baby-sitter but her husband has a job where he is able to come home to take care of the other children. She said, "Inevitably, when I get home from the doctor I am met with a barrage of anger. My husband implies it is my fault the child is sick, and he is angry because I've been gone so long."

When we must perform a service—for instance when this man knows they cannot afford a baby-sitter and he comes home to tend the children, it would be wise to do it with the greatest amount of grace that he can muster. He should do it lovingly, or graciously, or not do it in the first place.

It is obvious that this husband will have to undergo a growth period before the marriage will be a happy one, and such growth is difficult. He has developed these traits of character over a lifetime, but this husband can change if he desires to do so. Life is a school, and we have come here to learn. Some of us are now in the second grade, and some of us are in college, as far as character is concerned.

WILLINGNESS TO WORK

There is a book on the market today titled, *The Peter Pan Principle of Marriage*. I can give you the Peter Pan principle of marriage in one sentence: Some marriages peter out, and some pan out, and it is because the partners are willing to do certain things or else they are not!

My husband and I have been married for fifty-two years. When young people express awe and say, "You surely have been lucky," I reply, "Luck has nothing to do with it. A successful marriage comes about when two people have a willingness to do whatever is necessary to make their marriage work."

In one of the presentations I gave, I made reference to the fact that marriage is not a rose garden. At the conclusion of this talk, a young woman came up to me and said, "Do you know what? I think marriage is just like a rose garden."

I looked at her and thought, "You poor darling. Maybe you've been married such a brief time that reality hasn't set in."

Then she told me that she and her husband had moved into a house that was run-down and required a lot of effort to fix up, but was one they could afford. In the back yard was the evidence of what had been a rose garden—twenty or more rose bushes, that in their prime must have been perfectly beautiful. This young woman determined she was going to put forth every effort necessary to bring this rose garden back to its full bloom. She said, "What this required was that I get up early in the morning and water, spade, mulch, put weed killer, germ killer, and fertilizer on those rosebushes. My husband wasn't very supportive, because there were many things to be done inside the house, but I kept at that job. Then, one morning when I woke up early and looked out through my kitchen windows, one gorgeous rose had bloomed. I had never smelled a flower so fragrant or seen a flower so beautiful. My hands trembled as I cut it and placed it in a vase for us to enjoy.

"Now you see, I feel marriage is exactly like my rose garden. It demands a lot of work and real cultivation. It demands effort and time when your back aches and the sun's too hot and your hands get scratched. As far as I'm concerned, marriage is like a rose garden."

I had to say to that woman, "You are right, that *is* what a marriage takes. A marriage requires effort, knowledge of what to do, and the willingness to do it!"

What makes a marriage work? *Work* makes a marriage work. It is the determination to make it work. It is having a willing mind and being willing to pay the price to put forth the effort to *make* it work.

Sir Hugh Walpole said that the most wonderful of all things in life is the discovery of another human being with whom one's relationship has a glowing depth and joy as the years increase. The inner progressiveness of love between two human beings is a most marvelous thing. This cannot be found by looking for it, or by passionately wishing for it.

I totally agree. However, Walpole concludes, "Rather, it is a sort of divine accident." I do not agree. A marriage relationship that has beauty and depth and joy as the years increase is no accident, divine or otherwise.

The depth and joy are in direct relationship to our willingness to work and make the effort to do the things which bring joy into the relationship. And the effort must come from both partners. It cannot be one-sided.

Great marriage and family and interpersonal relationships do not just happen by "a sort of divine accident," nor are they simply the result of fortunate matches. Rather, they are the result of the work and effort and the will and determination of both partners to make the marriage great.

Small day-to-day successes take planning and work. These successes are not automatic. But the work can be fun. Taking walks together, trading the news of the day, making mealtime special, and a hundred and one little things we will discuss in other chapters make the difference between success and failure in a marriage.

Emerson said it this way, "Success comes by design, and failure by default."

~✗ 2 ✗~
Marvelous Differences

....

A marriage, any marriage, requires an understanding of the differences that will be immediately apparent when two people marry and begin to live in an environment that is the most demanding, intimate, frustrating, and rewarding relationship two people can ever experience.

Maybe those in my field have inadvertently given people about to marry some wrong ideas about marriage. Somehow maybe we have given the idea that if you have kept yourself virtuous and believe strongly in the principles of the gospel of Jesus Christ, when you are married, your marriage will be coming up roses all the time with no problems or differences at all. Of course, that is a fairy tale. No one was ever given a contract, or ever received any assurance that marriage would be a happy-ever-after affair. It simply doesn't work that way.

The person you have married is not a perfect human being and you are not a perfect human being. Here you are, two imperfect people with many differences. It is a wonderful and sacred responsibility to acknowledge the differences, to modify those that are modifiable and accept those you cannot modify or change. Therein lies real happiness in marriage.

It is true, there are many differences. In a marriage, there is a male married to a female, and there are tremendous differences between a male and a female. A woman is a woman. We look and talk and act and think and smile like a woman. A man is a man and he brings his own responses—those of masculinity. He walks and talks and acts and thinks and responds in a masculine way. Not that his way is superior to hers or hers superior to his, but they are marvelously different and we had better acknowledge these differences. Men respond differently in an emotional sense and they respond differently in an intellectual sense than a woman does.

Women and men even think differently about themselves. They see themselves differently. You watch a woman whenever she looks at herself in the mirror. She will carefully scrutinize her hair, and make-up or skin, straighten her clothing, smooth her skirt, and generally come to the awful conclusion that something has got to be done about something she sees.

A man rarely looks at himself critically. He is generally self-accepting. He gives the impression that he feels, "This is all I've got. I'm going to be happy with it."

Let me give you a little example. A wife might tell her husband in a loving way he is getting a little thick around the middle and probably should cut down on desserts. She says this because she is concerned, and the man will probably look in the mirror and acknowledge he is getting a little heavy. Then before he goes off to work, he may give her a little pat where she sits down and say, "Listen, sweetie, you could probably lose ten pounds yourself." Then he will go whistling off to work. He never thinks one more thing all day about that conversation. He probably eats pie a la mode for lunch and has a candy bar on the way home. What about his wife? All day long, she has probably thought about what her husband said. She looks at herself in the mirror intently to see if she really is getting fat. She gets all those articles out that tell how you can eliminate pounds, and she may go all day long without eating. She is in an awful state when her husband comes home. She has convinced herself she is going to pot; she is fat and unattractive. Her husband may grab her and give her a kiss and say something innocently like, "You're really an armful!" That little wife may burst into tears, because of her frame of reference, while the poor husband has no idea what he said wrong.

Yet these marvelous differences, when understood, can enhance a marriage. Why not sit down and acknowledge some of these wonderful differences? For instance, as male and female, you bring different backgrounds, different levels of understanding, and different emotional responses into the marriage as they relate to your disposition and temperament.

When my husband and I were invited to a very important social function in Salt Lake City, I bought a new full-length gown and gloves that went up over the elbow, because the party was very formal. The night of the ball, prior to getting into the bathtub, I put seven silver clips in the curls at the back of my head so they would retain their shape, and then I proceeded to prepare myself for the party.

Then, when I was all ready, I stood in front of my husband, who was also in his formal attire, and I said, "Now, Johnny, this is a very important party, and I want you to look me over very carefully, because I want to look my best."

He said, "All right," and very seriously, he looked at me from the top of my head to my toes, and then I turned around so he could see me from the back as well. After looking me over carefully, he declared with solemnity, "Sweetie, you look beautiful."

I, then, felt very confident, and we went to the party. We went through a receiving line, and we danced and exchanged dances with several different people. I felt it was a wonderful party. The hour was late when we got in the car and were on our way home, and as I sighed and leaned back on my hands, what do you think I discovered? I discovered seven silver clips in the back of my hair!! I rose up like a wounded bear and in my humiliation and despair I cried out, "Oh, no! Johnny did you see these clips in the back of my hair?" And do you know what my companion said?

"Yes, I did honey."

I wailed, "Johnny, why, why didn't you *tell* me?"

And with remarkable male logic, he replied, "Well, honey, I thought you wanted them there."

My feelings were almost bursting out at the seams. At that moment I felt we were not only different sexes, we were a different species! We must come from different planets! I was humiliated, and angry. I felt like attacking my husband, but I knew that if I did, he might not take me home! I struggled for control. I remained quiet the rest of the way to Orem, and it wasn't until we were in the house getting ready for bed that I was able to express feelings. I shared with my companion that *no* woman in her right mind would want to go out in public with clips in her hair. *No woman does*, I reiterated. I made my point clear, and he understood.

About three days later we were in Salt Lake City at the airport as we were leaving to take a trip together. As we stood in line, a well-dressed husband and wife stood about three people ahead of us. I noticed the wife had about four silver clips in the back of her hair. My husband also noticed them, and he got out of line, moved up to where this perfect stranger was standing, tapped her on the shoulder, and said, "Excuse me, you look very attractive, but I wonder if you know you have four silver clips in the back of your hair?" She looked at him in absolute astonishment, put her hand up to the back of her head and sure enough she felt all those clips in her hair.

In horror, she turned on her own husband, and said, with such anger, "Did you see these clips in the back of my hair?" Then she turned to my husband and said, "Thank you so much for telling me. That was the kindest thing for you to do," and she hastily extracted those four clips out of her otherwise chic hairdo.

My husband came back to where I was standing, smiling, really quite proud of himself, and he said, "Listen sweetie, I'm a slow learner, but when I learn, I learn."

Can you see that men and women are very different?

Another very obvious difference is the difference in personality traits. We have different personality traits not because we are either men or women but because we are individuals. Different personality traits are obvious even among the same sex and between twins. One may be talkative and the other quiet. One may be very orderly and the other one not. These are personality traits. We also have different talents and skills and differences in intellectual abilities and traits. Our schooling and our responses to teachers and subject matter affects our intellectual abilities. A woman is trained and educated to have some preferences and priorities in certain areas, while a man is trained and educated toward different skills.

What about our past experiences? Those play a great role in how we relate in our marriage. You have come from different homes. You had different mothers and different fathers, a different set of brothers and sisters and different grandparents. It doesn't matter if you grew up in houses beside each other on the same street, if you went to the same schools, and church—there are still tremendous differences because of the input you received from the homes you grew up in. Can you not see, in your marriage, the differences that are a result of having lived in different homes with different parentage? Even within the home, siblings will respond differently to the environment in that home.

Sometimes it's these very things—these past experiences—that will cause problems. We each have had different kinds of things happen to us—some good and some not so good, some frightening, some exhilarating—all of these things contribute to the sum and substance of us and we bring that into our marriage.

Then there are difference in lifestyles. We have different food preferences. One person may like enchiladas and another prefers baked beans. We have different recreational preferences. You'd be surprised how many times I hear some real complaints from men because they are married to wives who are non-athletic. Most men, I think, are inclined to be quite athletic and find pleasure in that part of their lifestyle while their wives may not.

I could go on and on identifying natural differences, not to mention all the specific individual differences.

Long ago there was a popular song and it went, "I like 'tomahtoes' and she likes tomatoes, I like 'potahtoes' and she likes potatoes and then the song goes on, "Let's call the whole thing off." And yet, that would probably be a mistake since those very differences may make for an enchanting and provocative marriage.

As a matter of fact, as you identify and acknowledge the differences between you and your spouse, you can see they can be a great enhancement to your marriage.

I'm going to share some differences my husband and I discovered very early in our marriage as we sat down and identified and acknowledged them. Number one, I'm talkative (which, I am sure is no surprise to you), and my husband is quiet. I overstate. I am flamboyant and my husband always understates. He is somewhat low-key. I am demonstrative and romantic and my husband is not—at least he finds it difficult to be openly demonstrative. He collects things and I throw things away. He is athletic and I'm more sedentary. He can never find anything—absolutely never—and I can find almost anything at any time, and I am (at least I used to be) a night person and he is a day person.

Now, consider all those things. We are genuinely different in numerous ways. Those differences have the potential of causing a great amount of conflict in a marriage, don't they? Let me tell you what we have done over the years.

First, I am talkative and he is quiet. That has been a strength in our marriage. As a matter of fact, I'm sure that I was drawn to him because of his quiet non-talkativeness. When we are together, and when we take trips, it is wonderful for me to have this quiet, introspective husband. He communicates well, but he allows himself to be a sounding board for me. It's very comforting and nurturing to me to be married to this kind of a man.

Maybe there are those of you who are married to talkative husbands and you are the more quiet and understated kind. But you see, the same principle applies. It's a difference, but it can enhance your marriage.

Now, he collects things, and I throw things away. This specific personality trait in my husband caused a few problems in the beginning of our marriage, and continues to do so, at times. He has a relentless need to collect things. I have followed this man in a green uniform around the world for thirty-five years. The military has sent us everywhere, and we had to be very careful and selective in the things we took, because we were allowed only so many pounds of household goods.

Inevitably, the thing that was absolutely necessary to take, as far as my husband was concerned, was this box filled with things that to me were pure junk—nuts and bolts and the strangest assortment of things. Whenever I would make the mistake of alluding to that as junk, let me tell you, I hit a nerve. With some forcefulness my husband would say, "How dare you call this junk? These are valuable things, and you never know when I am going to need these things."

Much to my chagrin, many times I had to eat the word "junk." My husband is a marvelous "fix-it man." He can fix anything. That's a wonderful trait. If something happened to the mixer or the toaster, he would go to this box of "junk" and he would extract a nut or a bolt or a screw and fix whatever needed fixing. Then he would say, "Ah, hah, see! If I hadn't had that box, this couldn't have been fixed." And over the years, I have acknowledged and accepted that while he collects things, he also fixes things.

I must add a post script. There are drawbacks to being someone who throws things away. There must be a law governing this, but I have noticed that as soon as I throw something away, the next day or the next week I have an overpowering need for the very thing I have thrown away!

Now let me tell you a story about our differences in being able to give affection openly. My family are Scotch-Irish. I have one brother, who is six years my senior. Therefore, I was raised almost as an only child, and we are a demonstrative family. Whenever I would leave the house for an errand, I would kiss my mother, dad, and brother good-bye, because I was leaving. When I came back I had to kiss them all hello. Does that give you the picture? That is my personality and my family experience.

My husband comes from a farm in northeastern Idaho. His mother is full-blooded English, his father full-blooded Swedish. The English and Swedish are more understated as a people, and his family is not demonstrative at all. When my husband received his first overseas duty assignment, and I shared with my mother and father that I was going overseas, and would be gone for two or three years, my family almost went into an emotional tailspin. My dad wept, my mother wept, my brother, my aunts, uncles, cousins, everybody wept. When we came home for the last visit, my husband was absolutely amazed to see all this emotion at my departure. I wept for a hundred miles after we left my family's home. Now, we went to his family's home. We shared with them that we were going overseas and would be gone for a long while. It made hardly a ripple. No one made any fuss at all. They said, "Well, isn't that nice?" or "Isn't that wonderful?" and the subject was dropped.

I thought, "They are not even going to miss us!" Then I thought, "No, they're hiding how they really feel, but they will fall apart when we leave." But we got to Pocatello, boarded the train, and they bid us good-bye. Still no one shed a tear! My precious mother-in-law was the last to say good-bye, and from her prim little English stature, she gave me a cold little peck on the cheek and said, "Good-bye." Then she gave her son two little pecks—one on each cheek—and told him good-bye as she turned on her heel and walked away without a single tear in her eye. I thought, "I cannot believe I have married into such a cold, unloving, unresponsive family."

I got on the train with my second lieutenant husband. He sat on one seat and I on the other facing him, next to the window of the train. I could see his face reflected in the glass, and he looked so sad. I had been married to him long enough I thought I knew what he was feeling. I reached across and took his hand and said, "Johnny, are you really hurting?"

He said, "Yes, I guess I really am."

I said, "Darling, I know why." And with that I jumped up and threw my arms around him and placed kisses all over his face and said, "Honey, don't you worry, I'll make it up for you. I really will. I'll love you so much you will never miss the love you don't have from your family."

As I sat down, he spoke. Evidently he hadn't even heard what I said, because he looked up and said, "Lucile, did you see how broken up my mother was?" I looked at him to see if he was putting me on, but he was serious. He knew something I didn't know—he knew that his family, no matter what, are self-controlled, and composed. They are low-key about the demonstrating of emotion. He knew what his mother was feeling when she kissed him and bit her lip as she turned and walked away. Though she didn't show a tear to us, he knew that after she was out of our sight, she undoubtedly shed some tears.

Even after all of these years, my husband finds it difficult to be demonstrative and open about his love and his affection. He loves very deeply, but he loves quietly.

These are differences in us. The differences have really enhanced our marriage in many ways, but only because we have come to understand and appreciate these differences between us.

What are some of those things, then, that are differences between you and your companion? Are you like the couple who was being described by a wedding guest when he said, "This marriage won't work. He's campfire, and she's microwave!" Remember, differences are to be expected. Are there some you can modify?

I mentioned that I was a night person when I married this man of mine, and he was a day person. I discovered that as a wife and as a mother who was married to a day person—one who begins the day with joy and whistling—and an early-to-bedder, if I could change my clock, it would be very smart to modify it. I began to modify by changing slowly but surely my ability to get up earlier in the morning. I have found over the years I have been able to modify my physiological clock so that I, too, have become more of a day person. I could see the wisdom in that because our whole society is built around people being day people, because those are the hours we can be more productive.

I've given you examples of differences acknowledged, or modified, which have enhanced our marriage. What about those things you cannot modify? There are things that you must accept. You must accept your mother-in-law and your father-in-law and the people in the family into which you have married. You may not feel loving and nurturing toward them, but you can change. The fact is that your companion has come from that family, and the more you accept his family, the better you will be able to accept him.

There are traits in your companion that you absolutely must accept because they will not change. I have had to accept that my sweet companion cannot see a thing in a drawer or in a closet unless it reaches out and taps him on the shoulder and says "Here I am." I have heard him say countless times things like, "Lucile, where is my blue shirt? I've looked through all the shirts, and I cannot find my blue shirt."

I might happen to know that the blue shirt is hanging between the tan shirt and the white shirt, and I will say, "It's hanging in the closet between the tan shirt and the white."

"No, it isn't," he will reply. "I've looked and I can't find it."

Of course, you know what happens. I go in the bedroom and sanctimoniously reach in between the tan shirt and the white shirt and there is the blue shirt! This is something about my precious companion

I have had to accept because it is obviously non-modifiable.

There is also something my companion has had to accept about me—that I am rather perennially tardy. I never get there for the opening hymn. If it's left to me, I'm never there for the singing of the Star Spangled Banner. This is a character deficiency. I know that. I have tried to analyze it in myself and modify it, but I have never been able to correct it entirely.

My husband is a very punctual man. As a military man, this quality is a real priority. My husband and I have gone over the reasons why I am late, and he has tried to help me overcome it. When I had children, I tried to allot the time necessary for me to take care of them, to get them dressed and myself dressed so I could be on time, but I almost never achieved it. We have decided that, evidently, I just don't leave enough time for the unexpected, like telephone calls. The telephone, to me, has such a sense of urgency when it rings that I just cannot let it ring. Have you ever felt that way? It could be the most important telephone call in the world, from a relative or a child. On the other hand, my husband has terrific discipline. When we are ready to walk out the door, no matter how incessantly that telephone rings, he just passes it right by.

My husband has accepted the fact that his wife will undoubtedly be late to her own funeral. It is something he has worked to accept and has done it in a gracious way, and I have tried to modify it as much as I could.

THE VERY REAL DIFFERENCES IN MALE/FEMALE NEEDS

In addition to our individual character traits, another thing we must accept about each other is the differences between the needs of the male and the female.

I have been married to the same man for fifty-two years, and for the last twenty-five of these years I have been a marriage counselor. From a review of my experiences I have prepared a priority list of the differing needs of an average husband and wife. These differences are very revealing.

A husband needs: (in order of importance)

1. Physical intimacy.
2. A recreation partner.
3. Admiration and praise.
4. An attractive wife.
5. Domestic support.

A wife needs:
1. Affection.
2. A husband who will talk to her and listen to her.
3. Fidelity and trust.
4. Financial support.
5. Spiritual and emotional support.

According to my findings a husband's number one need is for physical intimacy. Very often wives are not aware of this intense need. But it is wisdom for a wife to understand that physical intimacy makes a husband feel loved. Even if his wife does not see the experience as an expression of her love, he *feels* love when there is physical intimacy.

Men have no need to apologize for these needs—they are divine in their origin. However, men often draw faulty conclusions regarding the female's needs. Since Madison Avenue, television, movies, and magazines teach him differently, he may come to believe that all women are sensuous and provocative and desire physical intimacy as much as he does. But that is simply not true.

I hear men complain, "With all the millions of sensuous women, why did I get the one who isn't interested in sex at all?"

I always tell them. "Your wife is no different from most women. In surveys, women in general do not even list your number one need on their list!"

A husband's number two need is for his wife to be his partner in having fun together. He wants her to be with him in his recreation ventures, whether it be camping, fishing, at the ball games, or on the ski slopes.

My husband is an athlete and outdoorsman, and I'm really not. Skiing is something my husband loves to do and does well. He came from an area which is snow country, while I was raised in California not knowing the marvels of skiing. When we were stationed in an area where skiing was available, I felt myself to be a little old to be a beginning skier. I discovered, however, that it was important for him to be up in the mountains and in the snow country. In Europe when my husband skied all the Alps, I bought ice skates and learned to ice skate, because generally when you go to these areas, there will be places where one can ice-skate. I determined we were going to share winter sports, even if I did not ski, so we could be there together. We could go on the trips together, both bundled up in warm clothing, and at night, after a day out in the air—he on the slopes and I on an ice pond—we could talk and share.

My husband also loves to camp and hunt. He loves to be outdoors, and that had never been part of my lifestyle. As a matter of fact, though he likes to rough it, I must confess my idea of roughing it is to sleep on unironed sheets! But I have *become* an outdoorswoman for many reasons. As the children came along, I discovered camping provided fine vacations for us that we could afford. They were the kinds of vacations that were good for our children. They were training grounds—not only for our sons, but for our daughters. I learned early in my marriage that this was a difference between us, but it was a difference I could modify, and I have become a real pro over the years, and have come to enjoy sleeping in tents in sleeping bags, and being in the outdoors.

I say to women, you who are married to husbands who are outdoorsmen, who love to camp, and hunt, and fish, if those things aren't to your liking, share as many of your husband's sporting, athletic loves as you can so he will not need to go looking for companionship elsewhere.

Maybe you're very creative or artistic. Take along your knitting or your tatting or your easel and your oil painting. Or take your books, but do as many things together as you possibly can. It is one of the wonderful opportunities for bonding.

Men listed as number three their need to be admired and praised by their wives. Why? Perhaps one reason is that men rarely receive commendation from other men. A man is generally "under the gun," so to speak, having to prove his competence again and again. Women quite commonly say things to each other such as, "What a pretty dress," "Your hair looks great," "You make the best lasagna." Men rarely trade admiring comments. But even if a man is receiving plenty of outside commendation, the praise that means the most to him comes directly from the lips of his own wife.

Admiration does not even appear on the wives list. Perhaps the primary reason is not so much that her bucket of praise is adequately filled, but because her need is to be *loved* rather than just *admired.*

Number four on the list of needs for a husband is to have an attractive wife. Her weight, or her looks, is not exactly what these husbands were referring to, but the attractive qualities that caused him to fall in love with her in the first place—her smile, her enthusiasm, her demeanor.

Number five for a husband is domestic support. This means that he can come home to a clean house, food, some order, some peace. The message I hear most often is, "I need tranquility when I come home at night and some evidence of food being prepared."

One man said, "I feel a husband needs to learn to speak only two sentences in a marriage to survive. Number one, 'I love you,' and number two, 'Is dinner ready?' Surely if a man tells a woman he loves her, she will feed him!"

Notice, now, the difference in the list made by the women:

The number one need for a wife is affection, which is different from physical intimacy. Women are huggers. We hug each other, our children, and even the dog. But the person we most want to hug, and be hugged by, is our husband, because that is one positive way women feel loved.

A typical male does not have a strong need for this type of affection, but most women and children feel that affection is the cement of the relationship.

Affection sends the following messages to a wife:

"I'll take care of you. You are important to me. I don't want anything to happen to you. I am concerned about your problems and I am here for you."

Men need to understand how strongly women desire these affirmations. Hugging is a skill most men need to develop.

The second most important need for a wife is a husband who will talk to her and listen to her. I think most men know women like to talk. But a wife has a need to have her husband talk to her about real things, not just "Did you pick up my suit at the cleaners?" or "What's for supper?"

A wife wants to talk about the relationship, and to share her thoughts and feelings. This makes a wife feel close to her spouse. Men and women have different attitudes about what closeness means. Men say, "I want to do things with my wife, and all she wants to do is talk, especially 'trouble' talk."

Men often fail to understand how talking over problems can be bonding for a wife. Men want to find the problem, give a solution, and that's that! For example, once when I had a severe headache, I mentioned it to my husband. His only response was to suggest I take two aspirin. I replied that I had, and he said, "Well, take two more!"

That's not what I needed to hear. I needed him to ask, "Why do you think this headache is so severe? What happened today?" and then we could have talked about my problems.

The need listed as number three for a wife was fidelity and trust, which is not even on a man's list. Why? Doesn't he consider it important? Yes, so much so that he doesn't list it, he simply demands and expects it.

But many women need reassurance about their husbands' activities while out in the marketplace or on trips because they are aware of the attractive females their husbands are interacting with.

The number four need for a wife is financial support. A wife needs to feel safe. It is her innate instinct to have a home, a nest, a refuge against the storms of life, a place where her children are fed and warmed and where they as a family can feel secure. A tragedy of the modern world is the growing need for women to leave this refuge and seek a job in order for the couple or family to survive financially. I tell young couples to hang in there without that second income as long as possible, for the good of the children, if nothing more. What do children learn from TV or other children during those long hours while there is no guiding light at home?

Number five is the need a wife has for spiritual and emotional support from her husband—both for the family as a unit and for herself as his wife. Blessed is that union where a husband and a wife, and later, children, can pray together as a family tradition. This spiritual need of a wife is so listed because it has been at the root of discontent in many troubled marriages I have counseled. The husband is often so married to his job that he leaves the spiritual and emotional aspects of life to his wife. A marriage thus based has no cement and will fall apart under the pressure of other problems.

Have you, as a husband and wife, addressed these differences in your individual needs? What are those things that cause problems in your marriage that you have not accepted and so are beating yourself or your companion black and blue over?

One of the things I had a very difficult time accepting was that my husband liked only cowboy and western types of music and movies. I didn't like them at all. In the beginning of our marriage that was a problem, but we decided trade-offs could be made. As a matter of fact, we did a trade-off on several things that seemed hard to accept. My husband wasn't terribly fond of opera or the ballet, and I'm sure today he would admit that the ballet still isn't his favorite form of recreation or entertainment, but he has been loving and sweet and has gone with me to them, and I, in turn, have gone to his favorite types of entertainment with him.

While we lived in Europe, we had season tickets to the great operas in the area, and my husband brought his natural enthusiasm for good things to his understanding and appreciation of opera. He would read up on each one, and he became really more knowledgeable than I.

We have accepted the differences in our tastes as far as music and movies are concerned. I see some of his kind and he sees some of the romantic period movies I like. I listen to his kind of western and cowboy music, and he listens to the classics I like. Again, this has enhanced our marriage and broadened each of us considerably.

What are those things that you cannot seem to accept? List them, discuss them as honestly and with as little rancor as you can, and you will discover things you can do about them.

For all of the differences I have shared with you that exist between my companion and me, now let me share with you another list, a far more important list. These are the things about each other that are endearing, that make us compatible. I challenge you to sit down and identify for each other those things that are most valuable about your relationship as we have.

My husband and I make an excellent team. We admire each other. We respect each other, and we are absolutely, totally loyal to each other. We have fun together. We are best friends, and yet we both consider romantic love to be important and make sure it is a part of our lives. We like each other, as well as love each other. Perhaps most important of all, we have the same eternal goals.

When you have a list of those things that are truly important, then all of these can cancel out, in many ways, the little things that have been gnawing at your marriage, gnawing at your feelings about one another—differences that you have blown up out of all proportion.

The poet Samuel Taylor Coleridge said that men and women possess many qualities and the union of both is the most complete ideal of human character. He suggested that blending the like and the unlike is the secret of pure delight.

The marvelous differences that exist between a male and a female are there as part of being a man and a woman and a husband and a wife. Differences add depth and zest to our marriages.

When our children were visiting us this spring, we asked them, in a little family home evening, to identify foods they thought best described their mama and daddy. They concluded their mother was an enchilada and their dad was a baked potato. We laughed over that, but that is a pretty apt description. Johnny and I said, "You can add a dollop of sour cream to both an enchilada and to a baked potato and have a pretty fair meal. A whole meal of only a baked potato would be boring, and who would want to eat enchiladas all the time?"

A marriage is a contract in which the husband and the wife agree to work together to achieve eternal, God-given goals. Neither can achieve them alone. The contract involves innovations, creative problem solving, unity, unselfishness and much work. The differences in the partners offer the spice that makes everything else possible.

Identify those differences, acknowledge them, modify those that can be modified, then understand and accept the differences that cannot be changed. With that kind of realistic approach, your marriage will leap to the top of the heap, where our Latter-day Saint marriages should be!

~ 3 ~
Companions,
Not Competitors

....

There is abroad in the land today a lot of advice and philosophy that would have us believe that the male and the female are basically enemies. The philosophy contends that if a woman finds joy and contentment as a wife and a mother only, she is inferior, and not very competent or perceptive.

Too often I hear voices encouraging women to believe that if we want to be fulfilled and happy, we should be more competitive with the male. We should prove to him that we are, indeed, his superior. A women is encouraged to get out of her marriage, which is only a prison of sorts, and to get away from the home. If she has little children, she may parcel them out to day-care centers or nurseries so she can get into the marketplace where the action is and compete with the man.

I feel strongly that this kind of data, this relentless bombardment, is a dangerous thing. It leads women to believe in a basic falsehood—that men and women are competitors. A woman's role is not competitive with a man's role in any way; our roles complement each other. The truth is that men and women are equal, but they are not the same. It isn't that either sex or either role is inferior, they are just different. The French say, "Vive la difference," and I agree with that philosophy wholeheartedly. Scripturally we are told that the man is not without the woman, nor the woman without the man, in the eyes of the Lord.

I think of Adam who was not really a whole man until Eve was formed from and for him. It was then that he became a whole man. Heavenly Father told Adam and Eve to go forth and dress the Garden of Eden and have joy in it. Evil, in the form of Satan, very quickly moved into their garden home.

What happened next with our Father Adam and our Mother Eve? The book of Genesis in the Bible tells us Eve was beguiled to partake of the forbidden fruit. Nevertheless (and Father used that word—nevertheless) the choice was theirs. And the choice was made to break a commandment.

The third chapter of Genesis, verse sixteen, explains Eve's role to bring forth children. Father in Heaven, in verse seventeen of that same chapter, turns to Adam and tells him that his requirement as part of that transgression is to earn his bread by the sweat of his brow, all the days of his life.

When Father comes into the Garden he asks, "Adam, where art thou?" You and I know, of course, that Father, who is not redundant in any of the things he does, knew exactly where Adam was. Why then, did he ask that question? In that question, Heavenly Father acknowledges that he is aware of Adam and Eve's transgression. It is a very good question for us to ask ourselves—where are we? Where are we in our relationships, our marriages, with our companions and our families? It's very good for us to periodically take stock.

Father then turns to Eve and apprises her of the penalty. (She is addressed first because she was the first to transgress.) "I will greatly multiply thy sorrow and thy conception; in sorrow thou shalt bring forth children." I am the mother of five children, and as these children have come along and have grown, I've come to understand that labor pain is not solely what Father meant.

When our daughter was married properly, I thought, "Hallelujah—one down and four to go!" I have since learned that this was not the case. As a matter of fact, I added one more at that point over whom I would sorrow, and as each child has married and as the grandchildren have come along, I have been called upon to sorrow over *their* trials and problems. I now understand more fully what Father meant when he told Mother Eve that she would sorrow all the days of her life in childbearing.

Women, who are the nurturers of the human race, can appreciate what happened to me one night after we had received a letter from one of our older children identifying some problems in her marriage. I read that letter to my husband, and I was so weepy. We talked over the problem, and when we went to bed he was able to turn right over and go sound asleep while I got out of bed and wandered all around the bedroom. Pretty soon my husband opened one eye and said, "Listen, Lucile, those kids are grown, they must solve their own problems. There is not a thing you and I can do about it. Now you get back in this bed and go to sleep." Wasn't that wonderful advice? He turned over and began to snore. But it's not usually that easy for mothers to do that.

This is an example of the great difference in our roles in regard to emotions. There are some things that are peculiarly the female's strength and some which are peculiarly the strength of the male. Understanding this and accepting each other and our different roles is part of the secret of success in any marriage.

But these differences do not make us competitors. A woman is a woman. She walks like one, she talks like one, she thinks like one. A man is a man, who talks, walks, thinks and acts like one, and he is a man. They have these unique difference that were ordained before the world was. Men and women are not to be competitors. They are to be companions—to enhance one another.

The Lord ordained that the man be the head of the home and the wife be the heart of the home. We, as women, have the responsibility to learn to appreciate this divine concept of the male and the female as companions, and to place our husbands at the head of the home and teach our children to do likewise. That relationship has not been brought about by any mortal concept; it is the concept that God has ordained.

Someone has beautifully said, "It is not fitting that the man walk ahead of or behind the woman, or the woman ahead or behind the man, but because the woman was taken from the rib of a man, she should walk by his side."

These voices we are hearing which are encouraging women to be competitive are not new to this day. It is very interesting to go back and look at the various civilizations on which we have data. There are at least eighty-eight separate and distinct civilizations that we know something about. There seems to be a recurring theme in the decline and decay of these civilizations. They declined and now lie moldering in the dust largely because of the enmity that grew between the sexes. That recurring theme is the same one that the women of today are hearing. It was couched in a little different language, but the message was the same: To be a wife and a mother in the home is an inferior position, and women should get out in the world where the real action is and prove that they are as competent as the male.

As we follow down through the fall and decline of the Roman Empire, Sodom and Gomorrah, or any of the other civilizations which dwindled, we would see that the home became nonexistent, marriage was no longer a life-style, and the birthrate went down to zero.

Will and Ariel Durrant in their book *The Story of Civilization* categorize the similarities of some civilizations that have gone down into the dust and then compare those civilizations to the one in which we are living. The universal characteristic of each of these civilizations is this wedge or enmity that Satan has persistently encouraged between the male and the female.

I took three civilizations—the Weimar Republic, the Golden Age of Greece and the Roman Empire—and identified for myself some of the characteristics these civilizations had in common, which included the following:

1. The birthrate dropped.
2. Abortion and infanticide became acceptable.
3. Prostitution was legalized.
4. Homosexuals were recognized as a third sex.
5. Natural love between the sexes turned to hatred and violence.

Do you recognize any similarities to our day? Satan, from the very beginning, understood that if he could develop enmity between the male and female, the husband and the wife, he could win the war.

Today we see these philosophies infiltrating our society in a relentless and insidious way. There is much of violence between the sexes. We read about battered wives, battered husbands, sexual abuse, and physical abuse of all kinds and degrees.

Our hearts are heavy when we see and hear all these things, but we must remember Father is in the heavens. He knows the beginning from the end. None of this is a surprise to him. The Lord apprises us through ancient and modern scriptures what we can expect. Matthew 24 identifies in a most succinct manner the day in which we live. Jesus refers us to the words of Daniel for more information about the days in which we are living. Daniel refers to these as the times where "the love of many shall wax cold" (v. 12). So vicious and awful will these times be that "except those days should be shortened, there should no flesh be saved: but for the elect's sake those days shall be shortened" (v. 22).

What can we do? I would dare say that wherever you live today, that town or that state will not be one bit better than the homes that make up that community and state. The strength of the United States of America lies in the strength of our homes, not in our atomic stockpiles or even our armies, but in our homes. It has always been thus down through nearly six thousand years of recorded history.

Historically, we see that a nation can survive a multiplicity of disasters, war, invasion, and disease, but no nation has ever been been able to survive the disintegration of the family and the home.

General Napoleon Bonaparte knew this well. In the grim days in France long years ago, his generals came to him and said, "France is in trouble. We need better soldiers!"

Napoleon wisely replied, "France doesn't need better soldiers, France needs better mothers!" And if ever in the history of the world there were better mothers needed, it is now when there is such an encroachment on the roles of the male and the female, and upon marriage and upon the home.

Do not believe the voices today that say that to be a wife and a mother, to be involved only in mopping floors and changing diapers, is inferior labor. Wives and mothers have the opportunity to exert a tremendous influence for good in the world by staying in their own home and nurturing their families. There is no more worthy labor than influencing your husband and children for good.

You can be the one who makes it possible for this companion of yours and these children to perform the tasks that lie ahead. You, in large measure, can make them equal to it.

You will never do anything more significant, eternally, than what you are doing as the nurturer in your home. If you were the mayor or the governor or the President of the United States, I do not feel that you would be making decisions that would be as important and far-reaching as the decisions you are making in your home while you are raising those little children.

In a very great measure, the woman establishes the climate of the home. When a wife and mother loves her role and appreciates the value of it—when she stands with her shoulders back and her head erect, appreciative of the tremendous opportunity she has to affect generations yet unborn—she holds up that kind of a mirror to her family. Consequently the family can go forth into the world invigorated.

The husband who is kissed by his wife and told how much he is loved in the morning before he leaves for work, and children who are embraced by their mother and lovingly prepared for play or school, can go forth able to confidently accomplish the things that are needful that day.

The woman in the home is like the tide, and when she is in, all the ships in her harbor rise with that tide. When she feels dismayed and competitive and angry and resentful of her role, she is like the tide that is out, and then all the ships of her household literally hit the sandy bottom.

If you don't think this is a true premise, I challenge you to think about this. When you feel good, happy, and pleased about yourself, isn't it easy to influence your husband and family? Cooperation and unity are achieved almost without effort, and things just generally go well in the family.

When you are dismayed and disenchanted and unhappy about your primary role, or when you find it frustrating to be *just* a wife and a mother, it is communicated. Haven't you noticed your family can be up emotionally, but if you are down, very swiftly you bring the whole family right down to where you are and everyone in the household is soon grumpy and irritable?

How do you see yourself? Do you see yourself competing with your husband? Or do you recognize the wonderful division of labor, where the woman of the home as the nurturer, the psychologist, nurse, and teacher has the opportunity to exert unbelievable influence for good, *while* she supports her husband whose role is out in the marketplace.

Let me hastily add that I appreciate that there are many of you who wish that you could stay at home and cannot. Many of you are without a companion for whatever reason, and it is necessary for you to be out in the work force to put bread upon the table. You must indeed wear many hats. Not only must you make the living, but then when you return home, all of those roles that are generally women's roles are there for you also to fill. Only the constant support and help and assurance of a loving Heavenly Father can make it possible. Oh woman, if thou could see thyself, the woman that God sees, you would be absolutely thrilled with the opportunities that are yours. The Lord will make you equal to the task, if you ask for his help and rely on him for strength for your overwhelming task.

For those of you with husbands, keep in mind that men and women should be friends and supporters and be determined to help each other to rise to fulfill the measure of our creations. We do that by understanding our roles and supporting each other in our respective roles.

There is a wonderful story about Jimmy Durante, that great entertainer with the huge nose. He was asked to be part of a show for World War I veterans. He told the organizers his schedule would permit only a brief appearance. If they would not object, he would do a short monologue and leave immediately after his appearance. The show's director agreed happily.

But when Jimmy got on stage something interesting happened. He stayed and stayed, and the applause grew louder and louder. He was on stage for more than thirty minutes. As he came off the stage, he was seen with tears rolling down his cheeks. The manager asked him, "What happened? I thought you had to leave after five minutes?"

Jimmy replied, "I did have to leave, but I'll show you the reason I stayed. Look at the front row." Seated there were two men, each of whom had lost an arm in the war. One had lost his left arm, and the other had lost his right. Together they were able to clap, and that is exactly what they were doing—loudly and enthusiastically!

That is teamwork in spirit and action. Our process of becoming "whole" cannot succeed without our husbands. We need each other. Teamwork is what makes true love possible.

When husbands and wives work together and serve each other, a magic called synergy results. The word means the sum total is greater than the total of the separate parts. The word stems from the roots *syn* and *ergo*, meaning to work together. Thus a team can be far more powerful than the separate members working individually. It may be possible that one plus one can equal four, if we put our efforts together and move in the same direction in marriage, in the family, and in life!

Goethe said that a wife who is in competition with her husband, or who has just enough time to detect his faults, is the extinguisher of genius. She becomes executioner of her own power to give, encounter, elicit, and regenerate in him that which is of God.

I say boldly and without apology that men and women, husbands and wives, were not meant to be competitors. We were meant to be companions. And I declare with feeling and with joy that it is wonderful to be companions, not competitors. Our roles are splendidly defined, and we are to find joy in those roles. I would hope that you, as a woman, are marvelously womanly as you speak and feel and respond and act, so that it leaves your husband free to be truly masculine as he walks and talks and acts like a man, in the most divine sense of the word. You will then know the joy that comes from being companions and not competitors.

❧ 4 ❧
Spotlighting Strengths

I know a couple with a very unsatisfactory marriage, and it is not a secret to me why the marriage is unsatisfying. The wife keeps a book where she writes down what her husband has done that day to annoy her. She has spent all of her married years training herself to notice only the things she dislikes about her husband. That is a daily nail in the coffin for their marriage.

Think how different this marriage would be if she had a "love" book where she wrote daily the small, even trivial, things her husband did that made her happy!

I think of another woman who has a beautiful home. Her retired husband could usually be found working outdoors—fixing up, repairing, helping to keep the house and yard in good repair.

Although her husband took off his dirty shoes before he came into the living room, he always took off his old hat and gave it a toss in such a manner that it landed perfectly in the middle of the polished dining room table—leaving little puffs of dust as it landed.

This woman confessed to me that through the years this had caused her a great deal of anger, and she and her husband had even had harsh words over it, but he continued to throw his hat in the middle of the dining room table. This woman's foolish focus loomed larger and larger and spoiled an otherwise good relationship.

Recently I was visiting with my husband who had suffered a massive heart attack and was in the LDS hospital in Salt Lake City. I saw this same woman in the waiting room of the hospital and spoke to her. As she left she said, "Remember the hat on the dining room table?" I said I remembered, and then she said, "I would give all that I possess if tonight my husband would come into the dining room and toss his dirty old hat on the table."

"Well, go ahead and tell him so!" I said.

Sadly, she replied, "I can't. He died last month of a heart attack in this hospital. After the funeral I got that dirty old hat and do you know where I put it? On the dining room table! I wish I had known how happy I was."

In almost every encounter in life and especially in marriage, opportunities arise daily to focus on the positive or the negative. What we choose to do is critical to the success of our marriages.

It is not a matter of what is true or false. Choosing to focus on the positive side is simply a more effective and happy way to live. One of the primary things we can do to make our marriages work is to focus on what is good in the relationship—*not* on what is negative.

A woman in Portland told me that her husband died this summer of a heart attack. He was only sixty years old. He had been through a triple-bypass operation and seemed to be doing fine. He was able to speak and make plans for their time together after he got out of the hospital. Then suddenly and unexpectedly he died.

This couple had been married for thirty years. She had joined the Church twenty-five years earlier, but he never joined. She told me he was a wonderful man, but she felt she had been the light in their home and marriage because of her knowledge of the gospel and membership in the Church. It took his death to prove her wrong.

With his passing, she had discovered, *he* had also been a light in their home and in their marriage. It wasn't just her grief or loneliness that caused her to realize this, but a spiritual understanding and realization that came to her. But she was not able to understand and share this knowledge with him during their marriage because she had, she realized, focused only on what he *wasn't*, rather than on what he *was*. "What would have been, or could have been, the consequences had I done this?" she asked me pensively.

Perhaps there is no sin more common than the sin of faultfinding. Husbands find fault with their wives, wives find fault with their husbands. Children with parents, parents with children. Even in the Church it seems there are those who are constantly looking for faults in others. Faultfinders are never reasonable, logical, or consistent.

True, not all criticism is bad. There is constructive criticism, but there is a difference between being critical and hypercritical. Hypercriticism delights in criticizing for its own sake. It is a condemnation simply because of a difference in judgment. It is an exaggeration of matters of judgment or opinions. Faultfinding is being hypercritical.

Faultfinding is putting personal prejudice and personality in place of principle. It is so easy to drift from principle—determining *what* is right, to personality—worrying about *who* is right. Faultfinding is forming an opinion without all the facts. We must not judge without full information.

Faultfinding is imputing motive. While no court assesses a penalty for a crime until the motive is established, faultfinding doesn't try to understand the circumstances. Faultfinders are not willing to excuse or exercise mercy. They condemn the person instead of the deed.

In Galatians 6:1, Paul said, "Brethren, if a man be overtaken in a fault, ye which are spiritual, restore such an one in the spirit of meekness; considering thyself, lest thou also be tempted."

In other words, the spiritual person will help someone else to correct his or her faults rather than merely finding fault. The spiritual person looks at his own life, remembers that he is subjected to the same temptations as others, and contemplates what he would have done or said in the same circumstance—saying, "There, but for the grace of God, go I."

Usually those who are always finding fault with others are the most sensitive to criticism themselves. They are very often upset when mention is made (or even implied) of their own faults. In contrast is the spiritual person, who has removed the beam from his own eye and can now see clearly to help cast out the mote in a brother's eye. Paul is saying, "Let us help our brother get rid of his faults, but let us first get rid of our own!"

Utah has been my home, and there are some large and productive apple orchards there. I have learned from some of these farmers that something happens to a few of these apple trees, and for no apparent reason they do not produce fruit, they produce only wood and leaves. What does a farmer do in a case like this? I was stunned to learn that the farmer takes an axe and with a severe blow at the root near the ground makes a hole in the trunk of the tree.

The tree seems to receives the message, "Shape up and fulfill the measure of your creation or the next blow will severe you from your roots." Most trees will then begin to do what apple trees are supposed to do—produce apples.

We, too, sometimes need to have a shock in our lives to cause us to sit up and take notice and come to grips with those things we need to learn to be productive, fruitful trees.

A woman I will call Betty came to me to talk about some serious problems she was having in her marriage—problems which had been continuing since they had first married. Her husband, Bob, was very dictatorial. His word was law, and he left no space where she could express herself or disagree with him. Betty experienced bouts of anxiety and depression over this. She took her problems to the Lord. Knowing she couldn't change Bob, she asked the Lord for strength to cope.

One day in her scripture reading, she read the analogy of the tree and the axe in Luke 3:9, "And now also the axe is laid unto the root of the trees; every tree therefore which bringeth not forth good fruit is hewn down, and cast into the fire."

She went to the Lord and asked him if he would influence Bob with this scripture. She knew well the principle that Heavenly Father sometimes cannot answer our prayers because in so doing it would interfere with the free agency of another. Thus she added, "Thy will be done."

Betty said to Bob one day when he had said hurtful things, "I hope Heavenly Father will not take an axe to the root of our marriage one day." Bob looked surprised, turned white, and said, "Betty, sit down. I have just been reading the scripture about the axe laid to the root of the tree, and now you are quoting it, too."

For the first time Betty and Bob were able to sit down and talk about the problems in the marriage. Bob finally had *ears to hear* her. He, for the first time, had some *understanding* of what he had been doing. He wept in remorse as the Holy Ghost brought to his attention that he had exerted his priesthood authority unrighteously in his marriage.

Betty felt this was a miracle worth waiting for. The Lord honored Betty's request because it had not interfered with Bob's free agency. Would Bob have ever been able to accept this scripture as applying to himself if Betty had said, "Read this scripture and see what the Lord is going to do to you if you don't change!"

Now, however, Bob had been prepared to hear and understand. He said, "Betty, help me whenever I become a dictator. Just say to me, 'Remember the axe.'"

Jesus said, "Judge not that ye be not judged. For with what measure ye mete, it shall be measured to you again. And why beholdest thou the mote [or tiny particle] that is in thy brother's eye but considerest not the beam that is thine own eye?" (Matt. 7:1–3).

What does this mean? It means we will get back just what we give. As we do to others, they will do to us.

A man and his wife came to me with a list of their grievances and their problems. As I read them over I said, "Bob, with all of these complaints you have against Alice, I cannot imagine why you are still married." He pointed out that this was a temple marriage, and they had to think of the children, and Alice gave the same reasons.

I said, "I don't believe it. As I read all the complaints you've identified here, your problems are so horrendous that Church, the children, your families, none of these would keep you together if indeed your marriage is as bad and ugly as you have here identified. Now I want each of you to take two minutes and put the reasons you just gave me completely out of your mind, and I want you to come to some conclusion. Why are you still married? Why have you sought help?"

For two minutes they sat in silence, and then I asked Bob to address the subject. He said "Lucile, I can come to only one conclusion. I guess I really love Alice."

Alice spoke up and said, "I don't believe it! After all the things he has said to me and how he cuts me down!" She started a tirade.

I said, "Wait a minute, wait a minute. Tell me something specific as to why you think he doesn't love you and couldn't possibly love you."

She said, "All right. I'm going to give you an example that just took place day before yesterday that crushed me. I have really tried to lose weight. I know I am heavy and so I went out and bought myself a pretty nightgown, because I've lost a little weight. I brought it home and when he came home from work I showed him this nightgown, and . . ." Bob at this moment was looking humiliated, but she continued, "Bob said 'I don't like fat women in nightgowns.'"

I said to Bob, "Ooooo, that was unkind."

He looked at me and said, "I'm embarrassed over that, but let me tell you, if there's any justification, let me tell you why I said it." And then he told me about how he had worked for a long time to get an article published in one of the scientific magazines. When it was finally published, he was really excited, and he said, "I came home from work that night, and Alice was in the kitchen peeling potatoes, and I went in and said, 'Look! Look! I finally got this published.' Do you know, Lucile, she just barely looked at it and said, 'Oh, that's nice. Listen, will you take out the garbage?'"

See, we're tit-for-tat here. I hurt you and then you hurt me and so I hurt you back. Whenever you're in that kind of relating it is a no-win situation.

What I had this young husband and wife do was to think of things that could have been done or shared that would have been happy, positive things.

I said to Bob, "Now this week you have hurt her feelings, and she's devastated, but the week before she had hurt your feelings and you were devastated. Now, is there something that has happened in this past week you could have shared with Alice that would have made her happy? Something lifting? Something positive you could have come home with that she would have appreciated?"

He said, "Yes, as a matter of fact there is something I must admit I deliberately didn't share with her." It had to do with a new secretary in his office—evidently a beautiful girl—and the men were making appreciative remarks about her. He said, "One day last week I saw her as she moved over to the water fountain, and as she threw her hair back, I thought to myself, 'She has hair exactly like Alice—it's long and thick and shiny—and when she turns her head it's just like Alice does.'"

Alice said to her husband, "Do you mean you think my hair is pretty, and thick, and shiny?"

He said, "Of course, I do."

Then she said, "But you never tell me!"

He said, "Why, I've told you that."

She said, "When? Years and years ago, perhaps. You don't know what that means to me to have you look at a woman who is attractive and think of me. Oh Bob, I would have loved to have you tell me that."

Then, I asked, "Alice, is there something, perhaps, you could have shared with him and didn't that would have been lifting and nurturing?"

She said, "Yes. It happened last Sunday. Bob teaches the Gospel Doctrine class, and at the conclusion of the class three people came to me and said they had never heard a Gospel Doctrine class taught so beautifully, that Bob had explained a point of doctrine so well and in such an interesting way that for the first time they really realized what the doctrine meant."

When she said that, her husband jumped up from the sofa and said, "Alice, why didn't you tell me that? You know how uptight I've been about being the teacher in this class and I've felt like a failure."

We read in 3 Nephi 11:29 that "the spirit of contention is not of me, but is of the devil, who is the father of contention."

Most marriages begin with love, but by focusing on the negative we can bring contention into our homes. Our marriages can't proceed successfully and happily unless we learn to focus on the positive.

A young couple with two small children got into the destructive habit of highlighting only the negative they saw in each other. One morning the young wife said, "I cannot live like this anymore. I am taking the children and returning to my parents in California."

Her husband's reply was, "Good, the sooner, the better!" However, before she went, this young wife called her bishop and told him what she was going to do. He asked her to come and see him first. When she arrived at the bishop's office, he told her that he had called the stake president, and the stake president had called her husband and requested they both come to his office.

When the stake president had listened to them for an hour he said, "I know what you need to do, and if you are willing I think you can save your marriage. As your priesthood leader, I am going to give you a charge that for the next thirty days you stop this contentious faultfinding. I do not want you to allow one ugly or murmuring word to escape your lips. Whenever you have the inclination to say something cruel or unkind or demeaning, bite your lips, don't say it. Count to ten or count to a thousand, whatever it takes. Then replace those words with something that is positive, or lifting or loving. Reach back into your memory for the things about each other that you used to admire. My advice is that each morning as you arise, you speak words of love to each other."

The young husband stood up and said, "President, I object to this kind of counsel because you know that my wife and I don't honestly feel like that about each other."

The stake president said, "I am sure you don't, and I will tell you why. You have opened wide your doors and windows and invited dark forces to enter by your critical words. They are happy in your contentious home and contribute to that contention. How you feel now has nothing to do with it. We are trying to change destructive behavior. If you will take the assignment that from now on for thirty days you will strive to rid your home of these dark forces by speaking only positive words of love, you will find the positive feelings of love will come back. If you will do these things for thirty days, you will discover something wonderful has happened—the contentious spirit will have departed, and there will be love in your home once again."

That good young couple heeded the advice of their stake president. Today the marriage is intact. Is it without problems? Of course not. But they learned a lesson. This inspired stake president helped them learn about Dr. William James' great "as-if" principle. When you act as if something were true and speak as if it were true, it becomes true.

An army colonel's wife came to see me in Heidelburg, Germany, because she was angry with her husband and was contemplating divorce. She said to me, "Lucile, my husband has humiliated me in this military community for the very last time. I'm going to get even with him and hurt him as much as he has hurt me. I want out of this marriage."

I said, "All right, the first thing I want you to do is to go home and begin a campaign in your marriage to act toward your husband with every bit of love and appreciation you can possibly muster. I want you to cater to him, pray for him, and stop blaming him. Be as romantic and as provocative as you can be. Let your husband know he is the greatest thing since ice cream."

She looked at me like I had lost my buttons. In fact, that is exactly what she said, "Lucile Johnson, are you crazy? How in the world can I possibly do that, feeling the way I do?"

I told her the story of a ninety-year-old man who said he had been happily married because there were two things he had always done. Number one, when "Mama" (as he called his wife) got angry with him or was sharp, he said to himself, "Don't pay no attention to her. She don't mean no harm."

Then he said, "Number two, when we were married, my father-in-law gave me a watch, with an inscription which read, 'Say something nice to Sarah.' Every time I opened that watch to see the time, that is exactly what I did—I said something nice to Sarah, and that's why we had such a good marriage."

This colonel's wife looked like she was ready to jump all over me, and she said, "You want me to do those things, and yet I have come here for your help in ending this relationship?"

I said, "Oh, wait a minute. You are going to be able to end this relationship. But you told me you really wanted to hurt your husband. If you will do the things I have asked you to do, he will begin to be happy in this relationship, and when he is happy with all these things you have done, *then* you can hit him with the news that you are now filing for a divorce!"

She said, "Are you sure this will work?" I promised her it would. She left my office, and I kept thinking she would get in touch with me to tell me how things were progressing, but I didn't hear from her.

Then one day I saw her in the Post Exchange. I said, "Hey, Mary,

I haven't seen you for months. Have you gone ahead and filed for divorce?"

She had the funniest look on her face, and she said, "Lucile, you're not going to believe what has happened. I did all those thing you said I should do, and I have grown to care for my husband more than I ever thought possible. We now have the best marriage we have ever had. Isn't that strange?"

Of course, it wasn't strange at all, and just what I hoped would happen. What I wanted her to discover was that even though she did not feel loving and did not feel like praising her husband, and did not feel like being a romantic and provocative partner in her romantic life, she could do it. There is great power in this philosophy. If you want to change your relationship, you do the things that make a difference, and then the feelings will come.

If you wait for positive *feelings* before you do or say anything positive, you will wait until "you know what" freezes over. Just remember to tell yourself, "He don't mean no harm" or "She don't mean no harm."

Developing the habit of highlighting the things that please you rather than focusing on the things that disappoint you can make a significant difference in your marriage. This is also true with your children, your in-laws, your job, and your life.

TIMING, TOLERANCE, AND RESOLVING ANGER

In the ever-changing scenario of marriage, some things really never change. Whether you have been married three days, or three years, or sixty-nine years, your need to understand the principles of timing, tolerance, and resolving anger remain the same. These elements never change; they remain constant and important as a part of focusing on the positive.

Timing

Timing is an important factor in our lives and in marriage. We tend to criticize at the other person's point of vulnerability. But when the house is on fire is no time to complain about unmade beds. When you and your husband are out on the freeway and the gas tank has gone to empty and you sputter to a humiliating halt, this is no time to point out to him that it serves him right because he's always playing Russian roulette with the gas tank, and now he is going to suffer the consequences. This is not the time!

Regardless of how many years you have been married, the importance of timing remains constant. Beware of criticizing, of undermining another person at their point of vulnerability. This can be devastating to a relationship.

The Greeks have two words for timing and I think they're great. One of them is *chronos* and it comes from the same root word as chronology, which measures time as far as the day, or week, or the month. They also have another word for timing and it's called *chiros*, which means appropriateness.

Let me share a few little experiences. A young woman who had had some problem in her marriage called me one morning with some dismay. She and her husband had had a lovely Saturday morning. The children had gotten their own breakfast, and her husband had some leisure time that morning so they were lying in bed a little later than usual.

She lay in his arms with her head tenderly on his shoulder and the sun streamed through the bedroom windows to engulf them. They had been talking about things both large and small. It was a lovely, touching moment. Then her husband said with some sweet sentiment in his voice, "Elizabeth?"

And she said, "Yes darling," and looked up into his face.

He said, "Do you know you're getting a lot of gray in your hair?" What an inappropriate time to share this observation! She was shattered.

When my daughter, Paula, came back from her honeymoon, she called me and said, "Mother, this is the first night I will be able to fix Gordon's dinner, and I want to do something really special and really impress him. What can I fix?"

My daughter didn't have a lot of experience in meal planning so I said, "Why don't you fix that tuna-fish-noodle-mushroom soup casserole?"

She said, "Oh, Mother, that's such a plain and boring one."

I said, "You can put some pimentos in it to make it a little more colorful, and put almonds on the top. Make a tossed salad and have hot garlic bread, and set your table with candles and your new wedding linen and best china, and you be attractive, and Gordon will be so impressed when he comes home."

She said, "All right, I'll do it." About an hour past dinner time I contemplated my sweet little daughter having fixed her first meal so lovingly and having done it so well for such an appreciative husband. But the telephone rang and my daughter, obvious tears in her voice, began the conversation this way, "Mother, I hate Gordon!" That was not what I wanted to hear at all from my little daughter just home from her honeymoon.

Then she told me she had done everything I said and had this lovely meal prepared and Gordon seemed impressed. When they sat down to dinner, and he began to eat, she noticed he ate rather quietly. When he was finished, he pushed himself back from the table and said, "Paula, I am sure there has never been a tuna fish casserole prepared more expertly than this, but I don't want you to ever prepare it for me again, because there isn't anything in the whole world I hate more than this casserole." You can imagine what that little daughter did. She jumped up from the table in the proverbial bride's way and ran into the bedroom in tears.

I asked to speak to Gordon, and he told me that he really did hate that casserole, and he was afraid if he didn't tell Paula tonight, she would be feeding him that for the next fifty years. I explained to Gordon that I appreciated his feelings, but that his timing was poor.

Men often seem less sensitive to the appropriateness of timing than women are. I remember a story of a young bride who tearfully said, "I told my husband that there were two dishes I prepared the best of any—one was meat loaf and the other was potato soup." She said he looked down at the meal she had prepared for him and said, "Which was this?" Isn't that an awful thing for a bridegroom to say?

As bride and groom we lived at the Presidio in San Francisco. My husband was a brand-new second lieutenant and in those days when a young bride came aboard a post, she and her husband were royally entertained, by everyone from the Commanding General on down. At the conclusion of several weeks, the bride and her young husband were expected to return the courtesy and begin to have dinner parties in return.

I anxiously anticipated that at the conclusion of six weeks I would give my first dinner party. My husband and I planned the menu together. I said to my husband, "For our dessert I am going to bake that chocolate fudge sour cream cake I do so well."

My husband looked a little bit dismayed and he said, "Oh honey, I don't think you'd better do that. That really is a tremendous effort."

I'm sure he could remember the couple of times I had made that cake when the kitchen was an absolute disaster afterwards. That, of course, was before the days of cake mixes. And you talk about a cake from scratch, you'd better believe this was a cake from scratch, and it took a lot of effort and time, and I knew that. I said, "It's the dessert I do best and I'm going to do it."

He lovingly and quietly tried to talk me out of it, but the more he talked, the more determined I was to show him I could do it and so he said, "All right, it's your decision."

Of course, the day of the party everything went wrong. Only brides can appreciate that. The cake didn't get into the oven until very late in the afternoon, and as a matter of fact, many things were not done when my husband came home from work. He helped me set the table and do a lot of things, while I kept peeking at my prize cake in the oven. I ran upstairs to get myself showered and dressed. The guests began to arrive, and my sweet husband had to greet them, and I was getting flustered. Finally I got downstairs, and then excused myself to go into the kitchen to bring out my cakes. When I did, the hot pads were not properly protecting my hands, and as I reached in to pull them out, the heat on my fingers caused me to go "ooooo," and give a little twist and the pans flipped upside down. There was my prize chocolate cake in a million pieces on the floor. That was a point of absolute desolation for me. I felt like crying or screaming, but just then I looked up and there stood my young husband in the doorway. There were several things he could have done. He could have said, with some justification, "I told you, Lucile, I told you that this cake would cost you too much in effort and time and preparation and now look at what you've done!" But that young bridegroom said, "Honey, don't cry. Let's get some sauce dishes and we'll scoop up this broken-up cake and put some ice cream on it and serve it to them that way, and they'll never know the difference." That's exactly what we did, and the dessert was a tremendous success. It might be the original pudding cake!

I have been, for over forty years, absolutely indebted to that precious husband of mine, who at the point of my real vulnerability, came through for me with flying colors.

How many times do we find that when our spouse or one of the children has a talk or some presentation to give, and when the pressure is on and it is time to leave, the notes can't be found or the book can't be found, or a shoe can't be found? That is not the time for a companion to rise up virtuously and sanctimoniously and say, "I told you that you never prepare far enough ahead of time. If you had done this last night, if you had been more organized, if you'd have gotten all of these things together, then this would not have happened."

When someone has their back to the wall, so to speak, no one has to point out what was done wrong—the individual in question already knows only too well. What we need at a time like this is someone to be supportive of us in our moment of crisis. If you must point out a problem, do so later when your partner is not threatened, and try to do it in a loving way. Express the idea that perhaps it would help if they could do thus and so the next time to avoid repeating a problem. But timing is everything.

Tolerance

President Harold B. Lee in speaking to a BYU graduating class asked the students to be more tolerant of those who do not share their beliefs. He challenged the graduates to help diminish the intolerance which is responsible not only for emotional human suffering, but other ills which he went on to identify.

The same challenge could be issued to us in our marriages. There is an ugly war waging on this earth which is coming out in the open— the enmity between men and women discussed earlier. This is an evil that needs to be halted and replaced with tolerance for each other.

Alma tells us how we can do that, "having [our] hearts knit together in unity and in love one towards another" (Mosiah 18:21). Husbands and wives should be friends. Friendship is one of the grand principles that should infuse our lives. It should be a conscious desire and design for our personal fulfillment.

A man feels like a man when he knows his wife thinks positively of him and admires him. A woman feels more feminine when she feels loved, protected, and cared for. When she is so honored, this gives her a sense of belonging. When her husband does not put her down or compare her unfavorably with others and is kind to her, she feels more secure and feminine.

As a woman, I know that we are most susceptible to kindly words of love and appreciation. If a husband compares his wife favorably to other women and lets her know how fortunate he feels to be married to her, she will respond. I would tell a husband that his sweet companion's ability to respond and be loving and nurturing, in a great measure will be a result of how tolerant, loving, and tender he is with her.

Most of us are inclined in some respects to compare. We go to meetings or restaurants, and we see a husband and a wife relating well together. We might see a husband who seems so tender and loving, or maybe they sit in church and he has his arm around her shoulder. "What a wonderful marriage they have!" we may think. "I'll bet they never have a cross word."

You cannot ever judge a marriage by what you see when you are at church or the theater or a restaurant. You never know what takes place in anybody else's marriage in their kitchen or bedroom. The only marriage you can judge is your own because it is the only marriage you know. And you cannot compare your marriage to any other marriage that has ever existed. We will be judged only by what we have done in our own marriages with our own companions.

Your marriage will not be judged against the marriage of the stake president or the bishop or your Relief Society president or anybody else that ever lived, even against your own mother and father's marriage. The only marriage you will be judged by is your own.

Resolving Anger

Very often people ask me if I have drawn some conclusions about some problems that seem to be universal in marriage. My conclusion is that unresolved anger, anger that has not been addressed or recognized, is at the bottom of most of the problems I see.

Unresolved anger can destroy a marriage, because it causes physiological, psychological, and spiritual problems. I want to describe two couples who exemplify some of the consequences of unresolved anger.

A man and his wife came to see me, and this man had an unusually loud speaking voice. He was angry and verbal, and in the first session he said to me, "Listen, Sister Johnson, all of our problems belong to my wife." His wife, meanwhile, was looking very shy and hurt and even weeping a little. He continued, "If she can get her act together, our marriage is going to be all right." I thought it rather remarkable that he had already solved the whole problem, and I asked him what he perceived as his wive's greatest problem. He answered, "I'll tell you what it is. My wife is a cold and unresponsive, frigid woman. You tell her about her obligation to the marriage bed, and all our problems will be solved."

I had to tell that husband, and I share with any other husband that needs to hear it, that when a man has a loud voice, and an explosive temper, he intimidates his wife. There is no woman who can feel treasured and valued as a woman when a man speaks to her in this manner. Her natural tenderness and softness will change to withdrawal in such a situation. She may not show it because she has a fear of her husband's temper and wants to avoid any outbursts from him. She may not even recognize it herself, but most women will get even with the husband for treating her in this manner. Perhaps it will be subconscious but she often gets even by being unable to respond to intimacy.

In contrast was the husband with a cheerful expression on his face when we first met, who I soon discovered was a peace-at-any-price man.

His wife is a haranguer. She has belittled, criticized, and nagged him. But her nagging and harassment didn't seem to bother him. It seemed to just roll off his back. Soon, however, I found it had not rolled off his back. He had a lot of silent, stored anger and resentment, and this stored resentment had made his wife emotionally and sexually undesirable to him. Of course, he had not connected these two things, but his unexpressed feelings had very effectively neutralized his libido.

If burying anger or lashing out in anger destroys marital desire, then it is a problem of a very serious nature.I discussed with them the power of communicating like a two- or three-year-old child. Two-year-olds are masters of "I" language: "I want a cookie," "I don't want to go," "I love you," "I need to go potty." Two-year-olds never leave us wondering what they mean. We know exactly what they want and need because they tell us. That is what we need in our relationships. We need to learn how to express our feelings in a positive, direct way.

I have had men say to me, "The greatest complaint I have about my wife is that she is always angry, and she gets angry over such little things. She blows mole hills into mountains." As women, we have many things in our daily lives to frustrate us, cause us anxiety, anger, and hostility. When we approach our husbands with anger and hostility, we instantly cause our husbands to become opponents—we put them on the defensive. We need to ask ourselves if we are competitive when we strike out at our husbands over little things that are not to our liking? How can we overcome that so our husbands do not see us as negative and competitive? I believe we can learn to control these feelings of anger and hostility sufficiently so that we can share with our companions how we feel in a non-aggressive, positive manner.

Anger is always a secondary emotion. We may think anger is the first emotion we experience, but there could be at least one of four emotions that precede anger—sometimes all four at one time. These are fear, frustration, emotional pain, and physical hurt.

When people get angry with someone else, it is often because they see in that person a negative quality that they also see in themselves. When a fault in you provokes anger in me, then I know your fault is my fault too. If I have resolved and made peace with myself regarding that fault, then my anger will not be aroused by the sight of that fault in you.

When you find yourself feeling angry, ask yourself what you are feeling. Are you fearful or frustrated or anxious or hurt? Learning to recognize and express the *primary* emotion you are having neutralizes the anger. When we can express real feelings rather than anger, our partner's reaction is likely to be quite different.

Very often, in anger, we will use phrases that are like declarations of war, "You always do that," or "You never do that." This is a very competitive and negative stance. Instead, when you communicate, use "I" phrases. You may say something like, "I feel absolutely demeaned when you do that," or "I feel that I am not worth anything to you when you put me down," or "I feel hurt when you do that."

You are then sharing how you *feel,* and a person will not usually take exception to your *feelings.* These feelings are where you live, where you are. They need not be logical nor understandable, but we should not deny anyone his or her feelings.

"I feel" language is very valuable. As we share how we feel we can deflate and defuse anger. We are never able to change anyone else's behavior by anger, but we are able to change behavior in ourselves and others when we learn to express real feelings with "I" language—rather than using "you" language.

Wives sometimes tell me that their husbands do not accept their feelings and say things such as "How foolish of you to feel that way," or "How immature of you to cry. How childish of you."

A loving companion listens to feelings and gives his wife the right to feel however she feels.

What should a wife do if her husband says unkind things? When I was first married, my hair was long and black; today it is short and white. Today, if my husband had his way, I would have my white hair hanging down my back, because he likes long hair. Those are feelings, and I don't deny my husband his feelings, but every woman knows that long hair on an older woman is likely to be very unattractive and can make her look not only older, but as if she is trying to look young again. Therefore, I have had to encroach on his love for long hair in the interest of my own tastes and welfare.

One year we were going back to Boston for a family reunion at

Christmastime, and my husband was making it possible for all of our children to be there with their spouses. I went to the hairdresser and had my hair cut in what I thought was a short, but chic fashion. When I came home, I could tell immediately by the look on my husband's face that he didn't like my haircut at all, and he was very quick to so respond. He told me I had ruined my hair. Now, those were his feelings, and I didn't deny his right to have those feelings, but let me tell you about my feelings. I was devastated by what he said. I was really hurt. I had done something that couldn't be changed very quickly. The hair was already cut off. I couldn't paste it back. If I had bought a dress, and he didn't like the color or the style, and he felt strongly about it, I would have returned it, but what could I do about my hair?

He went on to make matters worse by saying that he was really surprised that I would make such a mistake as this. He said, "I would have thought you wanted to look your best when we go back to Boston." Is there a wife anywhere who cannot appreciate how I felt? I was angry and at the same time absolutely devastated. I felt he should have realized how hurtful it was for him to carry his criticism so far when it was something I could not change.

I had two alternatives here. I could have attacked him, and that is generally what we do when we are angry and have our feelings hurt. But when we attack we immediately have an opponent. So I chose the second alternative, I held my tongue and began to count until I could get my angry feelings under control. I knew I needed to wait until I could express my feelings without alienating my companion. It took me quite a long while to do this. I continued to work on my feelings while we got on the plane, and until we arrived in Boston. I was feeling a little better then, and felt I could talk to him about my feelings as soon as the opportunity arose.

It wasn't until after we had had a family home evening, and we were all snuggled up in a bedroom in that cold Boston home that I was able to share with him my feelings, as a companion and not an opponent.

I shared with him that a woman places an inordinate amount of importance on her looks—far more than men. From the time we are little girls, we are taught to look at ourselves critically. I shared with him how important it was for me that I be attractive to him, and when he didn't like the way my hair looked, I felt ugly. It didn't matter what anybody else said. I shared that I was devastated by what he had said to me, and how his words had almost ruined my trip. My husband was stunned.

Let me tell you why. Most husbands do not deliberately say things to hurt our feelings. They say things out of carelessness. Of course, our reaction is as if they did it deliberately.

My companion shared with me that he had no idea that he had hurt me or that my hair was that important to me. Then he went on to say some loving things about me, how he felt about me, and then he made this observation, "I think you would look wonderful, even if you were bald, like some people I know." Do you think my feelings changed?

Brigham Young gave some counsel which could help us as we learn to focus on the positive and overcome our tendency to faultfinding and anger. He said,

> When you are overtaken in a fault, or commit an overt act unthinkingly; when you are full of evil passion, and wish to yield to it, then stop and let the spirit, which God has put into your tabernacles, take the lead. If you do that, I promise that you will overcome all evil, and obtain eternal lives. (*Journal of Discourses,* 2:255.)

As much as we love each other, there are times when there is abrasiveness and ill feelings. When negative thoughts or emotions surface within us, we have the power to immediately let the Spirit take over and command these thoughts to stop. If we are in a place where we can say the command out loud, we should. It works well for me to precede the command with a good military group of words. The words are "Now hear this!"

As a second lieutenant's wife I learned about those words. I was told whenever I heard those words, "Now hear this," I'd better be quiet and listen, because they would be very important words.

When my husband and I were stationed in Yokohama, Japan, we had three little children and we lived on Yokohama Bay which was a dangerous tidal wave area.

One day at ten in the morning, my young husband called me, and after he greeted me, he said only these words, "Now Lucile, hear this!" I knew enough to keep my mouth shut, and that wasn't an easy thing for me. I wanted to say, "How wonderful to have you call. Is there any chance we could have lunch together today?"

You'll be happy to know I didn't say anything, I just waited, and it is a good thing I did because what I heard were very important, serious words. My husband said, "There is a tidal warning for Yokohama Bay. It is urgent that you take the kids—don't stop for one single possession—and just get in the car (a car that was always by prearranged agreement full of gas). Go to that highest spot" (also agreed upon by prearrangement just in case of an emergency like this). He reminded me again, "Lucile, don't stop for a single thing, because you are running for your life." I heard my husband, and we ran for our lives, and our lives were spared. That wasn't an easy thing to leave all our possessions I thought I would never see again. There were people who did not heed the warnings and instead ran for their things. They lost both their lives and their things.

When negative thoughts and negative emotions come, and they will come, remember the words, "Now hear this! I will not allow these negative thoughts, I want them to stop!" The other part of this process, of course, is to replace those negatives with equally valid but positive thoughts which will, in turn, bring about the positive feelings you want to have.

5

Joy Springs from the Little Things

....

What would you say if someone asked you, "Which is more important to you, your work or your marriage?" You would probably reply, "My marriage, of course."

However, the truth is that most of us give our outside commitments our best energy, attention, and efforts, as well as our best behavior. People outside our home usually get our politeness, kindness, attentiveness, and patience. In the home, we may not exhibit those same qualities. We spend energy on our career, the house and yard, and our church jobs. But how often do we spend our best energy, attention, efforts, and behavior on our loved ones? Too often we give our "best selves" and our "best time" to everything but our companion and our children.

Perhaps we need a little boost in our motivation. Think about it this way: If you had a company whose assets were valued at, say, five million dollars, would you leave any stone unturned to make sure you knew everything about this business? If you received a company report that advised you that your company was in trouble, financially or otherwise, would you think, "I'm too busy to worry about it"? Would you say, "I've got more important things to do"? No, you would bring every bit of effort and expertise at your command to make sure that this million dollar enterprise would continue to work, and you would even consider the little things that could possibly make a difference.

Or let's just suppose you had invested your savings in a little hamburger shop down the street. Wouldn't you make every effort and keep before you all of the knowledge necessary to make sure that shop would remain afloat?

Why then do we imagine that our marriage, the most important enterprise of life, should automatically be a success, that we can bring less than our best efforts to bear, think we are too busy or that we have more important things to do, and imagine the problems will somehow go away?

If our marriages are truly the most important enterprises with which we will ever be associated—and I maintain they are—then it is equally important we put the same kind of knowledge, effort, and expertise to this most important "corporation" that we would to making any other business succeed.

Will Rogers once gave a formula for success, and I believe it is pertinent in marriage. He said, "To be successful in life, whatever your endeavor, you must know what you are doing, you must love what you are doing, and you must believe in what you are doing."

Knowledge is power and we can gain knowledge of what to expect in marriage. One thing is sure, we can expect problems. It is said two things in life are inevitable: death and taxes. I add a third, *trouble*. Jesus himself assured all of us that we will have trouble when he says in John 16:33, "In the world ye shall have tribulation." (Shall is the Greek verb in the imperative mood: we *shall* have tribulation, in marriage, in our family and in our extended family.) Then he concludes, "but be of good cheer; I have overcome the world."

When trouble comes, and it *will* come, we should remember those words, as we contemplate on the purpose of life. The purpose of life is growth, and it has been said that there is little growth without pain.

Professor Bill Keaty is a law professor at the University of Pennsylvania. He begins his fall freshman class in exactly the same way each year. He has a large blackboard in front of the class with a number on each side of the board. The first thing he asks his class is, "What is the solution to this problem?" The students, of course, can't figure out what he means. Does he want them to add, subtract, or multiply these numbers?

Usually, someone will guess at an answer. Then, this professor says to the class, "You have not asked the key question. The key question is: 'What is the problem?'"

Then Bill goes on to say, "Not only in life, not only in law, but, in every endeavor, before we can solve the problem, it is essential to know what the problem is. If you don't know what your problem is, how can you solve it? You may end up polishing brass on a sinking ship."

I sometimes sit with people who have come for some kind of

counsel who are not able to identify their problem. They haven't even thought about what is causing their unhappiness—but they want me to fix it!

In order for us to put our knowledge, effort, and expertise into effect, we must first take the time to identify our problems. Then we can put our knowledge and expertise to work to solve the problems.

Richard Bach, author of the provocative volume *Illusions,* makes a great statement. He says, "Every problem has a gift in its hand. Solve the problem and you receive the gift." The gift may be a better relationship with your spouse or your children, or the gift may be peace of mind.

The reality of life is that life and marriage and parenting were designed for our growth, and there will be problems in all of these; but as we solve the problems, we will receive the gifts.

It is interesting to note that sometimes when we are not even aware of a problem, the Spirit will teach us in order that we can make corrections in our life if we are humble and willing to listen to the Spirit.

A perfect example of this happened when I gave a talk on the power of loving and empathetic communications and what this can do for a relationship. Afterwards, a stake president came up to me and confessed what had happened to him during my presentation.

He said, "As you talked about the power of communication, having patience, and taking the time to communicate, I felt quite smug. I thought, 'She's talking about the kind of a man I am.' I was sure there wouldn't be a person in my stake who wouldn't agree that I am a good communicator, and because of that I must be a great companion to my sweet wife. I looked over at her and was stunned to see her face because tears were shimmering in her eyes, and her lip was trembling. I couldn't imagine why my wife would be responding to your talk that way."

Then he said, "At that moment the Spirit taught me, and it wasn't a very pleasant teaching moment. I was told in those few seconds that indeed I was a good communicator and had all kinds of time and empathy for the members of my stake. But there would come a day when I would be released as stake president, as I would always be released from any church assignment I would ever have. But one assignment from which I would never be released, which was the most important assignment of my life, was as an eternal companion to this sweet wife sitting beside me. Did I always have the patience for her I had for other members of the stake? I did not. Did I always have the time and empathy for her I had for others? I did not. I stretched myself so thin with the members of my stake that when I got home, I didn't have any time or patience left."

He continued, "I felt very upset by that revelation, which made me recognize a problem I had not even been aware of. But now I recognize I have a problem, I am going to make some real changes in my life and in my marriage."

Most of the time, the things we need to do to solve our problems are not very convenient. In fact, they may be very inopportune, but if we are willing to pay the price, put forth the effort, and bring our knowledge and expertise to bear on our problems, something special will happen in our lives and in our marriages.

COMMUNICATING WITH CARING AND CONCERN

Let me share with you a story about a couple I counseled who had been married for twenty-seven years. Their children were either married or away to college. The wife revealed that one Saturday morning she and her husband were having breakfast together and her husband asked her to pass the orange juice. She couldn't hear what he said because he had the morning paper in front of his face. Twice she asked him what he had said, and finally he pulled down that paper, and in exasperation and anger said, "What's the matter with you, are you deaf?"

She said, "As I looked at my husband with his angry face, I thought to myself, 'I do not know this man. I am married to a stranger.' Such an overwhelming sense of fear and agony overcame me. I did not want to be married to a stranger."

How can a woman be married to a man for twenty-seven years and sleep with him all of that time, bear him several children, and then on a Saturday morning discover she is married to a stranger? It doesn't happen on a Saturday morning over a glass of orange juice. The strangeness creeps in in little and insidious ways.

How do these things begin? I believe it is through our failure to recognize that little changes that take place in each of us each day. They come about so imperceptibly we are not aware of it. Our faces change, our bodies change, our appearance changes, even the way we respond emotionally changes on a day-to-day basis.

Let's look at what may happen to each marriage partner as the years go by. Because the changes take place gradually and we may not be aware of what is happening to each other.

How many years down the road before a man becomes aware of the changes in himself? After a dozen or more years of marriage, perhaps when a man is in his forties, something takes place one day. He looks at himself in the mirror as he shaves his face and for the first time he is aware that maybe he has a little double chin or some gray in his hair he hadn't been aware of before.

A particular incident may have taken place that brought him to an awareness that he is not the man he used to be. He may play a game of tennis or badminton with a friend perhaps five years younger than he, and the man roundly defeats him. Or it may be that at the conclusion of a fast set of handball, this man finds out he is breathing heavily and is absolutely worn out while his opponent is ready for another match. It may come as an awful awareness of where he is in life. He is not as young and virile as he thought he was. Does he now begin to contemplate all the visions he had of setting the world on fire, being the president of a corporation, making a million dollars, or making his mark? As he's pushing forty or in his mid-forties, he realizes he is not going to do those things he thought he would, and it may be demoralizing for him.

At this same time, a woman is in the most demanding period of her mature life, because she still has the children at home—some of them young, some of them in their teen years. On top of family responsibilities are church and community responsibilities, and many women now work a full-time job as well, so there are tremendous demands upon a woman's energy and time. She is stretched and pulled and pushed every which way, with a real awareness of how needed she is. Because she has all these demands of a family, community, church, and perhaps job and aging parents, she may not be as aware as she should be of these doubts her husband is feeling about himself. Maybe she is missing his quietness and introspection, or other clues, because she herself is so busy.

This is one of those times when we really need to know what we're doing. By developing a little 20/20 vision, a little peripheral vision, we as a wives, can become aware of what might be taking place in our husband's mind, in his psyche, and with his emotions.

Husbands need to be aware that wives may be in the most demanding time of their lives so they can be patient if they are less than attentive—but that is not always the case. The men today, I think, *are* apprised in a rather factual way about the changes that take place in women in mid-life. It is pointed out that we have all these hormonal events taking place in our bodies and men are bombarded with books and magazine articles which warn them to beware of these changes.

However, it is important for a wife to understand and know that changes also take place in the male. Not so much hormonally, perhaps, as the changes that take place in a woman; but nevertheless, very real, unobtrusive changes take place in the male. Unless a woman is aware, unless she knows what is taking place and is aware of these changes and makes conscious decisions about what she will do in relation to these changes, she will come to the awful conclusion someplace down the road as my friend did, that she is sitting with a stranger at the breakfast table.

Marriage is a journey, it is not a destination. It is a constantly changing scenario, and therefore it is neither static nor passive. Rather it demands that we make continual adjustments in our course. We must know where we are going.

It is possible for married couples to share the same bathtub, the same bed, the same rooms, and yet have no idea of each other's thoughts and feelings in regard to day to day experience. Such marriage partners have lost contact with each other.

Deterioration of contact in marriage causes many marital problems. Lack of contact is the cause of more problems than adultery, money, or brutality. The loss of contact is deceptive; it creeps up on us.

When love is new it isn't difficult to maintain contact in our relationship. Each of us wants to know what the other is thinking about—their opinions, hopes, memories, and experiences. These things are exchanged eagerly. Unfortunately, this kind of contact doesn't always last.

One husband told me his wife was usually on the phone when he got home at night, and she would say something like, "Are you home already?"

The husband exclaimed, "At least my dog was happy to see me!"

How can we maintain contact so that our love is a moving force and not a static one? Here is an idea. We are all aware of the power of vitamins, and Vitamin C is especially important. I suggest that there are three vitamin C's of contact: communicating, caring, and concern.

One of the things you might do, as an exercise, is to remember how it was when you were first married. Do you remember all of the interest and curiosity you had in your partner, all of the dreams and the plans you shared when love was new? These things conveyed a powerful statement. They said, "You are important to me."

Perhaps as life has progressed and you have become engrossed in daily concerns, that contact and love has diminished considerably. You must re-establish your early belief that your partner's feelings and experiences are important to you.

Communication is a vital element in marriage. Even though husbands and wives may converse about the weather, other people, problems, and money, many never get around to talking about how to improve the marriage or their own happiness.

While many reasons exist for this lack of real feeling communication, too often *we* may be the problem. It might be very enlightening to ask, "Lord, is it I? Is it I who will not or cannot communicate on a feeling level?"

A sister came up at the conclusion of a program I gave and shared a poignant story with me. She said she had been married forty years, and her husband had just died. She was left a large potato farm and a generous insurance policy. She handed me a piece of paper and said, "But this paper is more valuable to me than all of that." I asked if she would explain, and she told me this story.

She had married very young and was taken immediately from her home in another part of Idaho to live in a two-room cabin her husband, Gus, had built on a homestead piece of land. It was far from the nearest neighbor, and even farther from a town, so she was lonely and homesick. She reached out to Gus for some words of encouragement and love. Each evening she would go to the fields to meet her young husband, and she would say, "Gus, have you missed me? Do you love me?"

He was tired and hungry and too impatient for "sweet talk," and his response was less than satisfying to this young bride. "What a silly thing to ask. Is supper ready?"

She learned from this that Gus could not, or would not, speak words of love unless it was in an intimate setting and they were in their bedroom. Within a year, business called him away from the farm. In the week he was gone, he wrote her a letter. She was thrilled because she thought he would tell her of his love and how much he missed her and couldn't wait until they were together again. But the letter was not a love letter. It was a factual description of his trip, and he concluded the letter with the words: Sincerely yours, Gus.

At that moment she realized the truth. Gus was not able or willing to speak of love, to share tender feelings. She hastily assured me he was a good and honorable man, and they had a good marriage, and a large family. Nevertheless, she spent forty years feeling cheated somehow.

Then Gus had developed a terminal illness which swiftly took him to death's door. Most of the time he was comatose. On the day he drew his last breath, he regained consciousness, obviously clear of mind and speech. With some urgency, he asked for a piece of paper and a pen. She gave them to him, and he wrote some words, then closed his eyes in death. The words? Only three: *I love you.*

I wish I could have counseled Gus. His inability to express his love could have been changed, and this could have brought such joy to his wife and to his marriage.

Many husbands, and some wives, do not have verbal skills when it comes to expressing tender emotions. However, it is a skill that can be developed. We can become experts in many fields when we pay the price demanded to learn the skills because we make the effort. Does learning to love, learning to verbalize or demonstrate love seem unimportant and not worth the effort? If so, your marriage may be at risk.

A bell is not a bell until you ring it. A song is not a song until you sing it, and love is not love until you give it! Speak the words you feel! Speak and act in the loving ways and the consequences will be enough to reinforce your actions.

I don't buy it when people say to me, "I know I'm not a good communicator. I never have been, and there's nothing I can do about it." Instead, I suggest a few things to consider.

Good communication is a two-way street. It takes two people who can both speak and listen. We don't tap into our partner's thoughts at the feeling level when we are talking about the weather.

Many people say to me, "What can we talk about? There isn't any new information. We've been married so many years, we know each other like a book." But they are wrong. Each of us is constantly changing, therefore, there is constantly new information.

Set aside some time regularly to talk about your relationship. Don't rush. You might ask a question such as, "What can I do to make you happier?" Even though we are each responsible for making ourselves happy, those significant others in our lives can do much to make us *happier!*

I suggest using some information-seeking questions to open the door to real communication. Sit close and touch one another when you are communicating. Questions such as the following have proven helpful in creating greater closeness:

1. Who were some of the most influential people in your life before you were twelve?
2. Why did you choose those three?
3. What were your most embarrassing moments? (Laugh together over these—bring a little humor into your caring.)
4. What was the happiest time in your life and why?
5. What was the most significant gift you ever received? Why?
6. What was your best vacation? Most fun vacation?
7. What are some of your phobias? (irrational fears)

A couple in counseling complained to me that their conversations very often turned into arguments. The husband had a pressure-packed job, and the wife was coping with four little children. Every evening each partner was looking for sympathy and support and solutions to the problems, but neither spouse had the patience to listen respectfully to the other one's problems.

When they should have been listening with understanding, they were marking time mentally, each wanting to jump in with his or her own complaints. I advised them to do some exercises to help them learn to be better listeners and told them that the act of listening might be the most important quality they could develop. I said, "Listening is far more important than anything you may have to say."

Listen carefully to what your companion says. Listening means paying attention to *what* is being said, as well as *why* it is being said. What are the unspoken messages that lie beneath the phrases that you hear? Whenever there is a tendency to disagree with what the other is saying, try using the words, "You may be right" or "Thank you for telling me." You have then opened the way for further clarification or feelings to be expressed rather than created an adversary.

Most of us are not good listeners. Let's take a look at why this is so. We can listen five times as fast as it takes a person to speak. In the time it takes a person to speak 125 words, we have brain-room for 600 words. What do we do with all that extra time?

We usually let our minds wander. We plan our next activity, or we perhaps think about what has happened that day, so we do not pay complete attention to the speaker. That is where the problem comes. If we would use this excess capacity of the mind to concentrate fully on what is being said, and perhaps analyze it, we could develop some real capability to listen with feeling.

If you are a bored listener, a selective listener, a defensive listener, or a non-listener, you are not listening with your heart. Because you are not listening sensitively you will miss out on some important things. You will miss out on feelings and you will lose closeness with other human beings.

We have a friend who told us this story. He was spading in his garden and upturned a worm. His five-year-old daughter was watching, and she was delighted. She leaned down and talked to the worm. One of the things she said was, "Jesus loves you."

The father, smiling, said to his little girl, "He doesn't look like he believes you, why do you think that would be?"

The child responded quickly, "Because he didn't listen with his heart!"

That little five-year-old already knew what most of us have forgotten—listening with our hearts is more important than anything we could say.

Are you a good listener? Are you ever guilty of ignoring what your mate is saying because you don't think it is very important? Or are you thinking about other things that certainly are more important? Divided attention sets up roadblocks to communication.

If you are "all here" then real communication can take place.

To listen another soul into relief and understanding, to listen another soul out of frustration, fear, and anger is one of the most caring and concerned acts of love we can perform with another human being.

Remember that the kind of communicating that establishes real concern and caring is in part non-verbal. One night at the conclusion of a family home evening with our five married children and their companions, my husband stood up as the patriarch of the family and said, "We're very pleased with you, our children. We love you, and we're honored by how you are conducting your lives, but your mother and I are worried. We are worried about the encroaching selfishness that can be seen in little spots in your lives. Selfishness can destroy an otherwise perfect union. Today it seems that society is caught in the 'What's in it for me?' syndrome. Everyone is concerned only with a partner meeting *their* needs."

Their father went on to say that a "me" philosophy will sow the seeds of absolute destruction in a marriage if we do not uproot it swiftly. He then talked about the other side of the coin and said, "Of course how you do that is with selflessness. Selflessness is being more concerned about someone else than with yourself. It is the attitude of 'What can I do for you? Help me to overcome the things I'm doing that are not pleasing to you.' These are the selfless qualities we need in our relationship."

After his counsel everyone was quiet for a moment, and then our middle son, who has a reputation as a wit, stood up and said, "Dad, I would like to make an observation here."

His dad said, "Great! Go ahead."

We all thought Bart was going to come up with something funny, but he was serious when he said, "I want you all to know—in all my life I've only known one truly selfless man." We waited, as he paused and turned to his father and said, "Dad, that person is you."

His father looked extremely pleased, as you can imagine. But I must have looked surprised because later that night when we were getting ready for bed, my husband said to me, "Lucile, I didn't like your response tonight when Bart said that nice thing about me."

I said, "Johnny, I never said a word!"

He said, "You didn't have to. You should have seen the incredulous look on your face." We have to be careful not only of what we say but also of our non-verbal language. Of course, I reassured my husband I was merely taken by surprise that Bart had taken that opportunity to express his feelings!

Good communication also helps us to pick up clues on ways we can be of help to our companions. In counseling, we sometimes refer to a Plinsol line. It's named after Samuel Plinsol, who was born in Bristol, England, in 1824. As a boy he used to spend time at the wharf watching the ships load cargo into the hulls. When he was a teenager, he made a discovery that some ships would overload and those were the ships that most often went down.

Samuel Plinsol later became a member of the British Parliament and authored the first Maritime Shipping Law in Great Britain, which determined exactly the number of pounds a ship could have in its cargo space. A line was drawn on the hull outside each ship with a black mark, and it was called the Plinsol line. A ship was permitted to fill its hull with only the amount of cargo that would cause the ship to sink into the water to that Plinsol line and no more.

In the field of counseling, we use that analogy. We need to be aware of our partner's Plinsol line in order to be sensitive to overload. When we are overloaded, things seem to happen to our personalities. Sometimes when a husband or wife's disposition changes there is nothing more seriously wrong than the fact that he or she is overloaded and exhausted. How will our companion know we are overloaded if we are not maintaining contact, if we are not communicating our needs to each other?

My husband is great in helping me keep from becoming too overburdened with obligations. Very often, he will offer to take the phone from me, and in his kind manner will say to a caller asking me to take on another assignment, "Lucile is really overloaded right now. She would love to do this, but at this time, she really can't. Would you be kind enough to call her at a later date?"

If we are communicating honestly, when overload occurs we will be able to recognize it and step in and help lift off some burdensome cargo from our companion.

Husbands are generally a little wiser in this area than wives, and a husband can rescue his wife when she gets herself overloaded. He can lift a load his wife is carrying and carry it himself or make sure that it is removed entirely, if possible. When the burden is relieved, the companion will usually return to her usual cheerful self.

When things are pressing in on us it is time to put into play the two T's—taking time. Take time for your companion. Make sure he or she is a real priority on your list. If you do not, you may come to an awareness that someone else took time to meet his or her needs, emotional and otherwise.

TAKE TIME FOR THE TENDER TOUCH

One of the most important things to take time for is the tender touch. I use the words "take time" because there are many things in our lives that encroach upon our time. The mundane, but necessary and time-consuming, things must be done—such as laundry, mopping floors, shopping, mowing the lawn, or washing the car—but these can encroach on the more important things. Unless we take the time, or *make* the time, for the "tender touch," such important things will go by the wayside and there will be regret in our hearts.

I have people who sit before me in a counseling situation and in sadness they will say, "If only . . . If only I had done that, if only I had said that. If only I hadn't . . ." But "if onlys" will kill you. "If only" is a dead-end street, but, as long as there is life and breath in you, you can change "if only" to these words: "Next time," words which give room for change and hope.

Take time for the tender touch. It is an important part of a whole relationship. It is, in fact, a validation of the relationship. A woman once said to me (she and her husband had been married seventeen years), "I feel as though there is a plate glass window between us. I see him and I see his expressions but I barely hear the things he speaks, because there is a coldness between us." Perhaps this coldness would not have entered their relationship if they had been aware of the importance of the tender touch.

POWER OF TOUCH

I was in Missouri not long ago, and one of the general authorities was also speaking in that area. He stayed with the stake president and had the stake president's master bedroom. He told us a story that illustrates the need we all have for contact with each other.

In the middle of the night the door opened and then shut again. When the door was shut, it was very dark in that bedroom. A small boy, about four or five years old, crawled into the bed. He must have felt something was a little different. His hands began to explore this general authority all over his head, up his face, in his ears. Suddenly, he realized this didn't feel familiar. He quietly got out of the bed and went to the door. Just as he got to the door, his mother appeared. The general authority wondered what the child would say to his mother.

The mother said, "You cannot sleep in that bed tonight. We have a brother from Salt Lake who is visiting, and he's sleeping there. You will have to go back and get into your own bed."

The little boy said, "But mommy, I'm scared."

His mother replied, "You don't need to be afraid, now you get back into your bedroom because there will be a ministering angel there to bless you."

In reply, the little boy said, "But Mama, I want to sleep with somebody who's got skin on him!"

We *all* need that "skin contact." There is a power in the touch.

I helped to prepare a letter that went out to five thousand married women throughout the United States—women from all social, economic, and religious backgrounds, women between the ages of about twenty and sixty-eight years of age.

We asked them one question and requested that they reply in

essay form. The question we asked was, "What is the one thing you would like to have either added to or that you believe would enhance your marriage relationship?"

What do you think the response was from women of all different socioeconomic backgrounds? Wouldn't you imagine there would be all kinds of answers? I was prepared for answers such as, "I would like my husband to remember my birthday or my anniversary," or "I wish he would be more romantic, or send me flowers," or many different responses. What was surprising was that most of those who responded did so in almost the same way!

These women responded that the thing they most wanted in their marriage was for their husband to understand their need to be held, to be embraced, to be touched with no sexual requirement. Isn't that interesting?

A husband usually feels that there is a hidden message when his wife asks to be hugged, and held, and kissed. What these women in the survey were saying is that "I want my husband to understand my need to be held and embraced and to have him be tender with me without it necessarily developing into a sexual response."

Dr. Mark Hollinder, of the University of Nashville, came up with almost the same data. He asked husbands, whose marriages were flat around the edges, "Has it ever occurred to you that your wife's persistent depression and anxiety may be because you are not holding her, loving her, and being tender enough with her without any specific requirement from her?" He challenged these men to ask themselves, "Is it possible that my wife is having a weight problem or a depression problem because I am not hugging her enough?"

WAYS TO SHOW AFFECTION

Hugging is a skill most men need to develop to show affection for their wives. It is an effective way to make deposits in a wife's Love Bank.

A husband can do other things to show affection. Perhaps he could send cards and notes expressing love, or bring his wife candy or flowers or small gifts.

A wife feels bonded to a husband who knows the importance of affection in its own right. Most of the affection women give and receive is not intended to be sexual. This confuses most men. Men usually want to skip the affection course and get to the main course. I hear men say over and over, "I'm not the affectionate type"—yet they are always interested in sex.

This is like the salesman who tries to close a sale by saying, "I'm not the friendly type. Sign here, you turkey. I have another appointment, so let's get this show on the road."

When it comes to sex and affection, women feel you can't get one without the other, but the typical male does not have a strong need for affection. Therefore, each husband should become aware of his wife's need for affection, and each wife should recognize her husband's strong need for physical intimacy.

I love to hold hands when we walk, but my husband hates it. He was in a military uniform for thirty-plus years and was trained never to walk touching another person. But in church we are great hand holders and have little squeeze signals that say all kinds of sweet things.

Wives, tell your husbands about the sweet and tender things he can do that represent affection to you. Is it a big hug in the morning, a kiss good-bye, a call during the day, or maybe a card in the mail now and then? You may think to mention how you like holding hands as you watch TV, or you may confess some particularly affectionate words you like to hear.

Husbands would do well to set a goal to practice some of these little things that show more affection for their wives until these actions become their ordinary way of relating.

Here are some ideas for enhancing closeness in marriage:

1. Take your partner breakfast in bed.
2. Talk late into the night about interesting things.
3. Rent a video, make some popcorn, and snuggle up to watch a movie you can laugh at together. Laughter is an aphrodisiac. Don't get a movie with emphasis on sex. That is a turn-off to most women.
4. Go for a drive to look at the city lights from a vantage point, and do some hand-holding with no hidden agenda.

To a woman affection is the environment of the marriage and physical intimacy is an event. You can't have physical intimacy all of the time, but you can have affection all of the time. It is the canopy that covers a marriage.

Take time for the tender touch, *make* time for the tender touch, and do it not only as husbands and wives but with your families.

When our children are little they are remarkably easy to hold tenderly and touch and embrace. But when these little ones grow up, and not always in the most delightful way—especially when they get to be cantankerous fifteen-year-olds—you know they're pretty hard to get close to. As a matter of fact, you may discover that you have some teenagers who are porcupines.

I have been quoted as saying that two of the paramount problems in life are when you have either married a porcupine or you have given birth to one! If you've married a porcupine, you are in trouble, because it is really hard to get close to a porcupine without getting stuck. But do you know what porcupines are saying? They are saying, "I need to be loved. I need to be touched. Just hang in there with me, please, because it is hard for me to let you fill my needs."

A man told me he had a humiliating experience at his work one day. His superior had dressed him down in front of his subordinates and unjustly accused him of an action. He said, "I was humiliated and wanted to tell him how I felt, but I need my job badly. I have a mortgage to pay and a wife and children to support, so I couldn't say what I wanted to say. However, I felt badly enough that I had to leave work early. When I got out in the car, I thought I was going to have a heart attack. My heart and chest felt like it was going to burst, and there was a lump in my throat. As I was driving home I thought, "What can I do to relieve this agony? I wish I could cry. But I was raised in a home where we were taught, 'Big boys never cry.' As a result, I don't think I've shed a tear since I was four or five years old."

He continued, "When I got home I decided I had to do something because I didn't want my wife to ask me what was wrong. I couldn't share with her yet. It was too hurtful, too raw. Still, I knew she would be aware immediately that I was home early and know from the look on my face something had happened. So I went in the front door, and slammed it, to let her know to give me space. Then I went into the bedroom and slammed that door shut to let her know doubly this was a bad time to approach me. I sat down in a chair with my head in my hands, and I hadn't been there sixty seconds until that bedroom door opened. I looked up and started to rise and was going to let her know she was thoughtless and insensitive to come in on me when I didn't want her to.

"But she never looked at me or even said a word. She just closed that door quietly and then moved around behind me, and with her soft, womanly hands began to massage my neck, and then my shoulders, and my back. There was not a sound except the ticking of a clock and those wonderful, rhythmic hands playing their magic as I felt the antagonism and humiliation and rage moving out of me. Then as she persisted in this loving touch, I started to reflect on what kind of a wife she had been to me. What a sweet and wonderful companion, the mother of my children. I continued to think about her and how tired she must be after being on her feet all day long taking care of the kids, yet still so willing to serve and love me. Thinking about her in this way and experiencing her loving touch in my life, do you know, before I could halt it, there rose to my throat a sob. It just escaped me."

Then he said, "On the heels of that sob, my eyes just brimmed with tears and flooded down my cheeks. I couldn't believe I could sit there weeping like this. She had heard the sob and felt the tears and she came around and sat on my lap. When she did, I noticed her own face was wet with tears she had been shedding all that time she had been massaging me, in that loving, gentle way—the only way she knew to tell me how much she loved me. She was hurting for me, but didn't know how to say it except with a loving touch."

He said, "There have been wonderfully intimate moments in our marriage, but there has never been one more profound than that one."

MAKE TODAY COUNT

People who belong to an organization named *Make Today Count* are people who are dying of a pernicious disease that will ultimately take their lives. The motto for that organization reads, "If I had twenty-four hours for living, the things that don't matter could wait. I'd play with my children, I'd hear all their stories, and I'd tell you I love you before it's too late."

We are talking about little things—little things in the relationship that can either make it or break it. One of these little things is the absence or presence of humor in a marriage. Some of our problems stem from the fact that we don't know the power of a lighthearted approach to life—not lightminded, but lighthearted.

I have two clients who come and sit in front of me, and they don't need to open their mouths; I can tell them their problems just by the look on their faces. Their faces are cast in cement. I mean, they radiate a grimness that makes me wonder if they have ever smiled in their lives. I immediately told them the importance of humor in the relationship—that humor is the oil that lubricates the machinery of the relationship. And I can tell you, as well, that we all must learn to laugh in our marriages or we're going to die. Many of us have learned that in many circumstances only humor can help or heal.

I knew a man pretty well who knew how to use humor. He and his wife have been married for a long time. She is a pretty good cook, and he likes good food, and it is her pleasure to always provide quite a delicious dinner at night.

However, it doesn't matter how long you've been married, sometimes you make a boo-boo, and this was her boo-boo night. The potatoes were underdone, the meat was overdone, it was really quite a pathetic meal. But to his ever-living credit, he never said a word. He sat there and ate every bit of that food. When she got up from a rather silent meal to clear the table, he jumped up too, put his arms around her, bent her over, and gave her a kiss that would not stop. Finally, when she came up for a breath, she said, "Darling, what did I do to deserve that?" And he said, "Well honey, tonight you cooked like a bride and I thought I'd treat you like one!"

When we read or hear about problems so infinitesimal as a cap left off a toothpaste tube, we think, "How ridiculous!" But it is the accumulation of little annoying things that we blow up all out of proportion which can cause disharmony and unhappiness in a marriage. Humor can help smooth out these little wrinkles.

A man and a woman who have been married for twenty-five years admitted that he never put the cap back on the toothpaste, and it drove his wife crazy. If I'd been able to counsel them early in their marriage, I would have asked him, "Hey, what is the bottom line here? Why are you punishing her? Why don't you come to grips with the real problem?" But, since they did not come for counseling, this problem went on for twenty-five years. Finally, on their twenty-fifth wedding anniversary, he decided that from here on out, since it had been so important to her, he was going to put that cap back on the toothpaste forever more. For a week he screwed the cap carefully on that tube. One morning at the end of a week, she eyed him very suspiciously and said, "What is your *problem?* You haven't brushed your teeth in a whole week!"

I am married to a man who has a delicious and delightful sense of humor. One day he said to me, "Lucile, after all these years we've been married I guess one of the things I love most about you is your sense of humor." Now, that was a nice compliment, but I really didn't want that to be one of the things he liked the *most*.

So I said, "Johnny, what about my intellect, or my looks, or what about this great body I have that would put Jane Fonda to shame?" And my husband replied, "You see, that's the thing I love about you—your sense of humor!"

I think about another time when my husband was building some storage units. His trousers were always dirty at night, and I would wash them for the next day. One of the little problems he has is that he never puts his money in his wallet. Sometimes on top of the dirty water in the washing machine I would find floating a dollar bill or a five dollar bill. Of course, if they had been hundred dollar bills, I wouldn't have complained!

One day I said to him, "Johnny, why don't you put your money in your wallet; that's where your money belongs." And his retort was wonderful. He said, "I'll tell you why. I'm always misplacing that wallet, but honey, I always know where my pants are."

A sense of humor will get you past some hard places in your marriages.

HAPPY MEMORIES

One woman had had some problems in her marriage. She was the mother of many children and my young friend had allowed herself to get too heavy and had not been careful as a housekeeper. The demands of the children literally inundated her. Until some serious things came to her attention, she was not aware of what had happened in her marriage.

One day her young husband said to her, "Since my secretary has been so helpful in the business at a very critical time, I would like to take her and her three children, and my secretary's mother, [they were both widows], to Disney World in Florida." He continued, "You complain about having us all under your feet, so I will take our older children, and then this will leave you with only the two smaller children. What do you think of that plan?"

My young friend said petulantly, "I don't care what you do." Then she called me for my response to what she said. Did I think that was the right thing for her to say? I told her, "No, I think it is the most foolish thing you ever said in your whole life." I continued, "You have made an error. You have given your okay for your husband to take another woman and her children, albeit perfectly aboveboard, to experience some happy memories with someone else, and that is absolutely a no-no.

"When you are allowing your husband to experience days that will be happy memory producers, you're very foolish to have those memory producers be with some other woman. I don't care her age or how attractive or unattractive she is. I've been married for forty years, and I would not allow my husband to go with any woman to have those kind of happy experiences. I'm going to be the one who is there with him."

My young friend said, "What do I do now?"

I said, "Make sure your house is clean today. Remember that is something your husband has complained about. Then put a good meal on the table tonight for him when he comes home. Make some plans so the younger children have been fed, and you can have a pleasant dinner hour. When your husband feels warmed and expansive, I would say, 'Honey, I have been thinking about this trip you are going to take with your secretary and her children and mother. I want you to know I would trust you from here to the ends of the world, there's no question of that. But I've thought about this. You're such a gorgeous hunk of a man, I would not trust any woman in the world with you. She just couldn't control herself to be around you, and I'm not going to put you into such a dangerous circumstance. How about taking me? Let's get a baby sitter for the younger ones, and we'll take our two older ones, and you and I will go together on this trip."

My friend on the telephone said, "Do you think he would like that?"

"If I were a betting woman," I said, "I would bet he will be overjoyed. You call me back and share with me what his response is."

When she called back the response was the one I had predicted. He looked pleased and said, "Do you mean you really think I'm attractive to women? You think women find me appealing?" He later told her he would love to take her to Disney World.

You see, the better part of wisdom, here, is to know what you're doing and to make sure that you and your spouse have as many bonding memories as you possibly can.

In our childbearing days there are frequent problems of finances and time. Husbands and wives are often associated only with things that are demanding—and the nickels and dimes and nuts and bolts of life—and our communication revolves around too many "Did you pick up my suit at the cleaners?" "Did you call so and so?" "Have you taken the car to be repaired?" We may not have as many happy, nurturing, touching experience as we should have. These are things we need for happy memories.

A couple came to see me, and their problems stretched for a mile.

All I heard was "This was wrong with her," "This was wrong with him." I finally said, "I'm aware of these problems. You've identified them for me, even written them on a piece of paper. But before we attack them, let's talk about some of the happy experiences you have had."

By the look on their faces, I could have assumed they had never had a happy experience in their whole lives, but I knew the man was an outdoorsman, and I knew they had been on some camping trips together. So, I said, "Tell me a little about any of your camping experiences."

They began to relate this experience and that experience and they told me something funny that had happened, and they began to laugh, and she recalled something he'd almost forgotten, and he laughed over that. Then he said, "Do you remember we did so-and-so," and she began to laugh about that. As a result, there was a loving, bonding feeling between them rather than a negative, angry feeling as we began to discuss the things that were wrong.

When you are down in the bottom of a pit, when things seem to pile in on top of you in your marriage, when you've grown apart and estranged and there's some distancing, you can do a thing that is very real and valuable and therapeutic. Sit down together—not to identify the things that have gone wrong—but first, to lay a foundation of those things that you can recall that were happy, nurturing, and nourishing. As you dip back, you will be warmed. As you renew together your memories you will feel closer and more able to cope with the problems.

AVOID BOREDOM AND MONOTONY IN YOUR MARRIAGE

Early in our marriage, my husband was stationed at the Pentagon in Washington, D.C. He took his lunch to help us save money, and I packed it every day.

That year we spent our leave on the west coast where my family and my husband's family were living. One day as my husband was talking to my father, I heard my name mentioned just as I was entering the living room. I stepped back a little to hear what my father and my husband were saying about me, and this is what I heard my husband say to my dad, "Lucile packs my lunch every day, and every day she sends me cheese sandwiches. I hate cheese sandwiches, but cheese is economical, so I eat the first sandwich, always hoping the second one will be a surprise, but it never is." Then I heard my father laugh, and make this statement, "Not having any surprises in our life can be pretty boring and pretty monotonous."

When we got back to Washington, D.C., and my husband took his first brown-bag lunch to the Pentagon, the first sandwich he opened was a cheese sandwich and he ate it, but the second sandwich he opened wasn't a cheese sandwich. It had a piece of cardboard in between two pieces of bread, and on that cardboard was written a message. The message said, "There is something provocative waiting for you when you get home tonight."

I am not implying you have to greet your husband wrapped in cellophane or any of these other things you hear about today, but what I am saying is this: whether it is in lunches, in menus, in your home, or in your clothing, be aware that if you love what you're doing and know what you're doing, you will make sure that boredom and monotony do not creep into your marriage.

I mention food because mealtime is the one time of the day that we can be together as husband and wife and children. I challenge you to put a little zip and zest into your meal planning. Candles, even for the children, make hot dogs more palatable. Use your ingenuity to add a little variety and interest to mealtime.

A very interesting story came to me from a young woman whose husband works night shift. Once in a while, she puts the children to bed very early and then gets them up about 11:30 and packs a lunch and takes the children and the lunch to the plant where her husband works. She has the receptionist call her husband over the intercom to tell him that his wife and children have come to kidnap him for a midnight meal. She shared with me that the children really get into this and her husband loves it.

Have you ever thought about having a fried chicken picnic supper under the light of the moon in one of the local parks?

One woman told me she took very seriously my suggestion to have something different. Though they had a patio, they didn't have any porch furniture, therefore, they sometimes took a picnic tablecloth out on that patio and spread a meal there.

Maybe we feel we have to fry a chicken or make potato salad in order to have a meal outside. Instead, we might be more flexible. Buying a loaf of bread and a piece of cheese makes a meal more spontaneous and takes a lot less time and preparation.

Speaking of variety and ingenuity, I suggest you use a little ingenuity in your clothing, particularly your night clothing, so that you are attractive and provocative. Women have a tendency to economize on their lingerie and other clothing so they can use the money for something for the house. Be sure that your clothing and your personal attractiveness are top level, not only for those meetings you will attend outside your home, but for that most important corporate president—your husband, within the home.

The better part of wisdom is to place all of the expertise at one's command into the relationship that pays the greatest dividends, not only now, but eternally. If we do this, we will be putting our efforts where "moth will not corrupt, nor thieves break in and steal." If we do not, we may find ourselves in a non-profit organization!

People who have successful marriages have learned the secret of the little things. They are aware on a daily, weekly, monthly, and yearly basis of the little things, such as changes in their companion and changes in their companion's needs. They take the time to put an emphasis in their lives on those things that are nurturing and lifting and happy-memory promoting. They are aware of the little things from which joy springs.

As one observer put it: "When I contemplate the tremendous consequences that come from little things, I am convinced there are no little things."

Section Two

The Ups and Downs of Mothering

~❧ 6 ❧~
Your Best Is
Good Enough

....

FIRST, THE DOWN SIDE

Motherhood can be a demanding, frustrating, often thankless task, as the husband of one of my clients learned firsthand. I'll refer to the couple as Ken and Joanne.

Ken was a very successful young entrepreneur. Ken and Joanne had five children, three of them preschoolers. When Ken would come home at night, he was not very pleased with the way Joanne kept the house. As a matter of fact, he thought she was a pretty poor excuse for a housekeeper. The first thing he would say almost without fail when he came home was, "What have you been doing all day?"

One day when he came in and there were lots of toys and clutter strewn around, Ken said, "What is your problem? Why can't you keep this stuff picked up?" Joanne looked at him tearfully as he continued, "Let me tell you what your problem is, Joanne. Your problem is lack of organization. Everything in life can be handled by the principle of organization. If I ran my office the way you run this house, we would be bankrupt." To add insult to injury he added, "By the way, I have a secretary who is great at organization. I ought to bring her in here. She could teach you some things."

Joanne was simply cut to the quick, but the next morning she had a plan. When Ken went to work and the older children went to school, she told the three younger children they were going to have a little vacation. They could stay in their nightclothes if they wanted to, and they could do as they pleased all day.

They all had an absolutely marvelous time! Joanne read magazines and ate snacks, and the children ate graham crackers in the living room, spread their toys all over, and had quite a day. The mess from food preparation was not cleaned up. Everything was left right where it was used. Not a single dish was washed, not a floor was swept or mopped, not a bathroom taken care of, not a bed made.

When Ken came home and saw this mess, he nearly exploded. "What have you been doing all day?" he raged. But this time Joanne was ready for that question.

"Absolutely nothing! Absolutely nothing that I usually do every day, and this is what would happen if I didn't do *every day* all the things you don't give me one bit of credit for."

But Ken wasn't convinced and he replied, "I want to tell you something, Joanne. I could run this house as smooth as silk, with one hand tied behind my back."

This gave Joanne an idea. She said, "All right! Let's just trade roles for a little while, and I won't even require that you have your hands tied behind your back. I've had business training. I'll get up in the morning and run your office for a week, and you stay here and run the house."

Ken laughed. "Great! I need a vacation!" and together they set out the stipulations of the things he would have to do at home and the things she would do at the office.

Joanne told me later, "I just couldn't wait. Imagine being able to get up in the morning and get dressed up and get your hair all done and leave that tacky house and all of those kids, and get to go to a nice clean office and eat lunch at McDonald's every day!"

Ken added, "I was excited, too. This would be such a wonderful object lesson for Joanne. I was going to prove to her that the name of the game was *organization* and besides, I was planning all these extra things to do with all the blocks of time I could create."

At the end of the week, Ken's words had changed significantly. They were so poignant that I wrote them down. He said, "I battled constantly with sticky fingers, dirty noses, dirty bottoms, quarrels, and spills. My clean windows were soon smudged, my freshly mopped floors soon dirty. There was jelly on the refrigerator, peanut butter on the chairs, even ice cream on my new stereo! One day when the children were particularly quarrelsome and uncooperative, to my horror I heard myself saying, 'You just wait till your mother comes home!' I knew the time had come to take off my apron and to welcome back my dearly beloved genius of a wife and mother and homemaker."

Well, you can imagine that Ken never again asked Joanne what she had been doing all day. In fact, in his repentance process, he penned some words so beautiful that I submitted them to a national magazine for publication.

"There is no job in all of the world more overwhelming, more taxing, more relentless, more frustrating, and more thankless than that of a wife and a mother and a homemaker. To realize that it is done so well by so many who know and appreciate their awesome responsibilities is the greatest tribute that could ever be paid to another human being." And I say *amen!*

DOWN WITH INAPPROPRIATE GUILT

Very often I have distraught mothers say to me, "Oh Lucile, I've made such mistakes in my role as a mother." I remember one sweet stake Relief Society president who wanted to talk with me. She was the mother of five grown children who were married in the temple, sons who had been on missions, etc. She was a remarkably successful woman, as far as I could tell. Yet she shared with me, with some pathos, that she and her husband had been taking a class on marriage and parenting and that she was so depressed because she had made every mistake in the book . . . every mistake! She said, "Obviously, I'm a lousy mother. There are so many things I've done wrong."

I had to kind of smile, and I went back over the information about her children who seemed to be very outstanding, well functioning human beings, but she persisted. "But, Lucile, really . . ." And then she went on to explain some of the things the class had made her realize: "I should have done this, and I shouldn't have done that. I should have said this, and I didn't say that, and the class just keeps pointing out all the errors I've made."

In my experience, most mothers feel exactly as she did. I do not personally know one solitary mother who thinks she has done a great job as a mother and is totally satisfied with her job performance.

I talked to her about how hard we are on ourselves as mothers. We read articles and attend classes, and we are apprised of the things we should be doing and the things that we shouldn't be doing, and, of course, up against ideal pictures and philosophies of parenting most of us fall short!

I said, "Of course you made mistakes and will continue to make them, but remember you did the best you could in the past with what you knew at the time, and you are still doing the best you can. God himself will not ask more of you than that."

I want to share with you, as I shared with her, that being a good mother is just making more right decisions than wrong decisions, and that you should be a little kinder to yourself, a little more generous to yourself. And how about being a nurturing parent to yourself too?

In a Fast and Testimony meeting in Lethbridge, Canada, a young mother tearfully confessed, "I have overdosed on drugs and I have been suicidal. My depression has been so black, not because I lost a home in a mud slide, like some of you have, but because of little things—such as my little girl not being potty trained, my husband not being affectionate, my older son being rude, or the weeds taking over the garden and five pepper plants dying."

Self-pity and depression are often the results of inappropriate guilt—one of the primary sins of mothers. It was the bottom line in this mother's problem. She unconsciously felt she *should* be able to have her daughter potty trained, she *should* be able to get her husband to be more affectionate, she *should* be able to teach her son not to be rude, and she *should* be able to keep the garden weeded. When she could not control everything around her, she felt guilty and incompetent when she was actually doing the best she could.

Many mothers seem to wear guilt like an old bathrobe that is too familiar to discard. Mothers, don't beat yourself with guilt and regrets. Perhaps you "yelled a lot" or "nagged a lot." So, you yelled and nagged. Is there a mother alive who hasn't done both? But did you love those children? Did they, and do they, know you love them? That is what really counts.

One way to conquer inappropriate guilt is to make friends with a pad of paper. Whenever you feel distressed, overwhelmed, depressed, or angry, write down your feelings using a free-flowing handwriting and descriptive language such as: "I feel angry. Why do I feel angry? I am depressed and lonely. Why do I feel like this?"

Pull out all the data you have in your computer brain and write about it. Be expressive, be dramatic. Ignoring or denying feelings won't diminish them, but writing them down often will. Putting our feelings into words often helps us sort them out and get rid of the inappropriate ones.

Counselors call this type of writing "emotional vomiting," and it is very healing. It gets negative feelings out of your system and cleanses the body and mind. However, you may want to scribble over each line to make the words unreadable or tear the paper into bits and throw it away after you have finished writing. You want to get the feelings out, not recycle them by reading them over. Women are naturally gifted as healers. Use some healing on yourself—you deserve it, and you will be a better mother because of it.

NURTURING YOURSELF

Our middle son was eight years old when we lived in Maryland at a military post. My husband felt he was lucky to be the branch president where every sister was so gifted. Each had wonderful homemaking, mothering, and teaching skills. It seemed they had it all.

I felt very inferior, especially to the sister who lived next door because she was a wonderful cook, and that was not my strong point. This sister baked bread and pies and cakes that were truly awesome. One summer evening, my eight-year-old Bart and this next-door neighbor's daughter were talking on our back porch and I overheard Nancy say, "I bet you wish you had my mother instead of yours. She made us the best supper," and Nancy began a recitation of delectable food they had just consumed. I could just imagine Bart's mouth watering, for I knew mine was. Then Nancy asked, "What did *you* have for supper, Bart?"

There was a silence and then dear, loyal little Bart, who couldn't recall a single delicious dish said, "Well, my mother is very nice." How I cringed! I worried too. Would Bart grow up scarred because he had no memories of hot baked bread or lemon pie?

The next day when I was taking Bart to Primary, I said, "Bart, when you grow up, what will you remember about me?" During the silence I thought accusingly to myself, "Just as I suspected. Bart is growing up scarred and wounded. What a terrible mother I am!"

Then Bart snuggled over close to me and said, "Mother, I will remember you always smelled so good."

I was surprised and pleased. As the miles rolled by I thought, "Maybe, just maybe, that is almost as good as remembering the smell of freshly baked bread." I realized that my little son was really saying he had spent a lot of pleasant moments being close to me!

No wonder I have since advised: Go ahead! Buy perfume, bath powder, and bubble bath for yourself and use them—you deserve a little pampering. At the same time, you are giving your little ones more reasons to want to be close to you. You never know when you will make a memory that will linger for years.

Women are nurturers to their children, to their companions, and to everyone else—even their own mothers, and their mothers-in-law, and the neighbors. But they are often at the bottom of the totem pole when it comes to *being* nurtured. Too often they forget to nurture themselves. They don't know how to ask for what they need from others, and they don't know how to give themselves credit for what they do right. You should recognize that for the most part you are undoubtedly a very good mother indeed.

PRAYER—YOUR FIRST RESOURCE

When we become parents, we are given the wonderful responsibility for the welfare, the care, and the spiritual, physical, and emotional well-being of a child. However, we are given this parenting role without any previous experience. We weren't born with a PhD in parenting. Why do you suppose that Heavenly Father has so decreed that we become parents without any previous experience? I think it is because he knows that in our desperation we will be on our knees where we need to be seeking him, pleading for patience, forbearance, and understanding.

In missionary work, what is the first thing an investigator is asked to do without fail? *Pray!* Sixty-three of my counseling clients who admitted to a diminished testimony and faith listed as the number one reason: "I didn't want to pray."

A major area where Satan will work on you is to beguile and persuade you to let your prayers slip and then let them go completely. When the regularity of your prayers decreases, your spirituality begins to diminish. As mothers, we cannot afford to let our prayers slip. When you pray regularly and sincerely, your heart will not be troubled. You will not be afraid, and you will have peace of mind.

I remember a woman in Napa, California, who came up to visit with me after one of my talks, and she told me she had nine children. I asked her how she kept her balance with that much responsibility, and she replied, "I just mop and pray, and wash and pray, and clean and pray, and cook and pray!"

I think our parenting is a little bit like a story I heard about a father who was driving through the night with several of his small children in the car. At one point he fell asleep at the wheel for a few seconds. When he awoke, he felt the presence of a guardian angel riding along with them and steering the car gently. Our parenting role is something like that. We become exhausted and may even fall asleep at the wheel. But we are given more help from above than we may realize.

One of my clients, a convert to the Church, is a student at BYU. In speaking of his background, he said, "I came from a home of poverty— such unbelievable poverty you cannot imagine."

I nodded compassionately, picturing some kind of a tenement house in California. Then, to my surprise he said, "Our home cost $250,000, and our cars were Lincolns or Cadillacs. My mother always had a maid. I went to private schools. We vacationed in Hawaii or the Caribbean. My father is a prominent doctor."

Then he continued, "But I had never prayed in my life until I was a grown man and the missionaries taught me how. Prayers were never a part of my home life. So you see how I came from a home of poverty? My life totally changed when I learned how to pray!"

Mothers, you may not live in a home of affluence, with maids to do the dirty work. Perhaps you only dream of vacations to Hawaii and designer clothes to hide your lumps and bumps. Your home may be filled with worn and spotted upholstery with rugs to match, and your car may be a Volkswagen bus. But if you are a mother in a home where *you* pray, and you teach your children to pray, you can count yourself wealthy and among the truly spiritually affluent!

Make the Lord your primary resource. Do not rely on the so-called child care authorities or feel they are privy to some kind of inspiration or knowledge that is kept from you. That is not true. What I could give you as a rule of thumb is this: Compare what you hear from "experts," or what you read in books, to the gospel of Jesus Christ. If the information does not conform, then you have absolute authority to forget it because it is simply someone's opinion, and it will not survive.

When you will do your praying first, and then go to the authorities, and the books and the lectures or whatever as *secondary* resources, appreciatively and properly putting what you hear in the context of the gospel of Jesus Christ, you will then make more right decisions than wrong decisions. That is what good parenting boils down to—making more right decisions than wrong decisions. There are no perfect parents, only parents who make decisions, do the best they can, and learn and grow in the process.

A CLUE FOR SUCCESSFUL PARENTING

In parenting, as in life, the scenario is constantly changing, and therefore there are no sure-fire formulas anyone can give us to help us be successful parents. However, if I could give you one clue for successful parenting, as the scenario changes in your parenting, I feel it would be that your child, regardless of his age, never outgrows his tremendous need for assurance that he is a worthwhile human being and a person whom you love. Your child needs to know he is loved, without any question or any doubt. Your child needs to know that with surety, and he needs to know that your love does not depend on his behavior or the grades he makes, or the things he does.

In 1979, a tough-acting juvenile was brought into the probation offices where I was counseling. He swaggered in and acted like a really tough kid. Juvenile offenders are allowed one phone call. When I asked whom he would like to call and suggested that perhaps he would want to call his dad, he emphatically said, "No. I want to call my mother."

The boy broke down in tears on the phone and sobbed his heart out, "Mom, I want to come home!"

Because he was a member of the Church, I decided to talk with the boy privately until his mother came. He said, "I will never do this dumb thing again. I can't believe I could hurt my mom so much. She doesn't deserve it."

"What about your dad?" I asked.

"Oh, Dad's never around. He's so busy and involved, he doesn't know what's going on in the family, and I really don't think he cares. But Mom does. Oh, she yells a lot. She nags and she's always on my back, but I'll tell you one thing. She cares! She really cares about me and what happens to me and that means a lot. Do you know what she said on the phone? She asked *me* to forgive *her*. She was sorry she had failed me somehow. I was supposed to *forgive* her? Forgive her for what? For being a mother who loved me when I don't even deserve it?"

Loving our children—even when they don't deserve it, even when they are not acting lovable—is what mothering is all about.

When babies are little and pliable and amenable, oh, it's easy to love them, isn't it? It's so comforting and such a simple exercise to love that sweet little bundle—all those toes and all those fingers and all that softness and sweetness. As you bathe, diaper, and feed him, you're expressing in a dozen different ways, "I love you, you're so special."

Though your baby does not know those words, your love comes across in a very real way. Your voice and your eyes and your touch as you clutch him to your shoulder and to your breast, and snuggle your lips against his ear—all those things say to that little baby, "You're a wonderful person." The baby internalizes all this love and acceptance even before he can understand what you are saying.

However, babies have a way of growing up, and becoming not so lovable, and not so delightful. When that happens, we are inclined to step back, especially when that little baby grows up to be a mouthy and cantankerous teenager. That teenager may begin to question our brilliance, and let us know we don't have all the answers at all. As a matter of fact, our value judgments and a lot of other things may be questioned. This may make it much more difficult to love in a very demonstrative way. Especially if we try to embrace and love that human being and are rebuffed. How many mothers have attempted to put their arms around a teenager only to have them say, "Mom, stop it, that's kid's stuff. I'm too big for that."

If you hear that enough, you can't help but feel like backing off. But, don't do it. Remember that the one thing that never changes in the changing scenario of your parenting is your child's need for love that is expressed both visibly and verbally.

EXPRESSED LOVE CAN MAKE THE DIFFERENCE

I once counseled a teenage boy, who was in trouble with the law. He did not respond favorably to counseling and was insolent, sullen, and withdrawn. His father, an impressive-looking general, agreed to join us in what was to be our last counseling session. When he came into the room with his son, the tension and hostility fairly crackled between them.

This father was openly critical of his son, and I felt I had reached an impasse. In one final effort to make contact between them, I turned to the father and said, "Let's lay our cards on the table and tell it like it is. I guess there is nothing about this boy you like or respect. You just don't care for him at all."

The father looked as though he had been struck; then bristled with anger. Then, this great big general got up, pulled his skinny teenage son to his feet, and with an emotion-laden voice said, "Son, I want you to know I love you!"

An electric silence filled the room, then the son dissolved in tears, and threw his arms around his father's neck. "Oh, Dad, why didn't you ever tell me?"

The father replied sadly, "I wanted to, son, but I was afraid it would make a sissy out of you." This boy, whose problems were based on his feelings of being unloved, ceased to be a troublemaker.

We need to take the time and make the effort with our young people, to embrace them, to let them know how much they're loved and how special they are. The more difficult and unlovable a person is, the more evidence you have of how greatly that person needs your love!

When children reach the teenage years, they go through a transition period which is not easy. They have one foot in the child's world and one in the adult world, and they are probably a little scared. They may feel alienated and isolated and are probably the loneliest people in the home. They usually have little confidence in themselves but put on a good front and act like the classic "know it all." We love these clumsy, irritating human beings, but they often do not believe that we do. Therefore, we must show them and tell them.

Teenagers do not interpret critical comments as constructive discipline, but as lack of love and caring. Furthermore, when they hear negative statements about themselves and their character, they believe those negatives. As a result, many teenagers are unnecessarily susceptible to the loving overtures made by cultists, drug dealers, and others who succeed at first in making them feel important, cared about, and accepted just as they are.

For example, recruiters for the Unification Church, often called Moonies, have been very successful in recruiting American teenagers. After studying their standard operating procedure, I learned that in the beginning they are loving, accepting, and physically affectionate with the young people they are trying to recruit. They are very successful in influencing these teenagers because many of these young people come from homes where they have not felt loved at all. They may have heard only things like, "You're so lazy. That's the dirtiest room I've ever seen in my life! Pick up your dirty clothes. Your hair looks awful." Although their parents may have loved them and simply been trying to teach them correct behavior, the negative manner of the parent's teaching made the teenagers feel rejected.

Of course, after the initial "loving" overtures by the cultists, when the teenagers are officially part of the organization, they are cruelly brainwashed. They may realize, too late, that this is not the love they were seeking.

There is only one way to decrease our children's vulnerability to such manipulation. Whether your child is two or twenty-two, you hang in there. Never let a day go by that you don't, in some way, get your arms around that child or hold that child's hand or shoulder. I don't care if your son is six-feet-two and has just come in smelly from a football field, you grab that kid, even if you have to grab him around the knees. When you get your arms around him, tell him you love him because that is the only way he knows he is loved. You know you love him, and the Lord knows you love him, but make sure *he* knows you love him.

Our kids need, not only loving words, but some good, old-fashioned "bear hugs." Let's go farther than putting hands on each other's shoulders and touching cheeks. That is what I call an "A-line hug", which is not very satisfying because we're not touching much of each other. We may lean over and pat each other on the back in a "burper hug," but that is not what we need, either. We need the "bear hug" kind of hugging, loving, and touching in our families.

How about the "sandwich hug?" Dad can be a piece of bread, Mom can be a piece of bread, and you can put the kids in the middle. One of them can represent a piece of bologna, and another one can represent a piece of cheese, and you can build yourself up a great, big Dagwood sandwich as you love each other. And you know what? You'll laugh and maybe even fall down on the floor together.

LOVE IS NOT COMMUNICATED WITH "THINGS"

You might take exception to my premise that love must be verbalized and demonstrated and say, "There are many ways we already show our love, and many ways our children are apprised of that love." What are the ways you would say you show your love?

One father was dismayed when I told him his sixteen-year-old girl had assured me she was convinced he hated her. He said, "She couldn't think I hate her, because of all the things I've done for her." He listed for me the shoes and coats and all the other things he had bought for her.

However, your sons and daughters do not equate your loving them with the things you buy for them—the clothes, the food, the house to live in, the school tuition. Neither do they equate the things you do for them with love—the floors you scrub, the bread you bake, or even the chocolate cakes you make for them. It's a very unusual child who would ever go to a dresser drawer and pull it out and say, "Oh, Mom, thank you for all that clean underwear. Now I know you love me." As a matter of fact, there had better be clean underwear in there because, as far as they are concerned, that is your job. You don't get any brownie points for that.

Dads work out there in the marketplace all day long and bring home money so they can pay the mortgage so the children can have a roof over their heads and can buy all of those expensive shoes, but dads don't get any brownie points for that. Children believe that is just expected. They point out that is a father's thing. They do not equate those sacrifices with love at all.

That may seem very unfair, but unfair or not, it is true. Your child's rationale is, for the most part, that as a father and as a mother, the law would force you to put a roof over their heads, would force you to put bread in their mouth and shoes on their feet. I've heard teenagers say to me, "Why, animals in the jungles take care of their own."

There will come a day when your children will be able to understand that the things you did, the sacrifices you made, and the things you bought them were indeed evidences of your love. But that appreciation does not generally come until your children have reached a considerable maturity, and usually not until they are married, and are buying shoes or scrubbing floors for their own kids. Then they are more inclined to think, "This is what Mother and Dad did for *me*. I never fully appreciated all the things they did."

CASE IN POINT—
A PEPSODENT TOOTHPASTE SMILE

We were stationed in Aberdeen Proving Ground in Maryland when our oldest daughter was fifteen years old. That is quite an age. If you have children that are fifteen years of age, you have my condolences. I call it the hiccuping period of adolescence. Hang in there, because it will pass.

Our fifteen-year-old daughter had crooked teeth, which meant that she needed braces. We were stationed at a post where there was no orthodontist. This meant we had to go to a civilian, and we had to pay a lot of money for his services. We could ill afford it, but we felt it was important, so we sacrificed, and we took this fifteen-year-old and drove her all the way to Baltimore to have braces placed on her teeth.

Was she appreciative? Not one bit. As a matter of fact, she protested. It was a battle. She wept every time we came back from one of the occasions when she had to have the wires tightened on her teeth. She was a most unappreciative child, but we felt very virtuous about the sacrifice we were making for her. We knew we were doing it for her own good.

One night at dinner, when we were in what I lovingly refer to as that "hour of peace and rest," this teenage daughter began to tell her father and me all the things that were wrong with us. If you have a teenager you know that is par for the course.

She identified many things about us that she just couldn't tolerate. But the coup d'etat was this, "Dad, why is it that you drive the oldest, most dilapidated, car on this entire post?" Then she went on to explain that all of her friends and their fathers had much nicer, newer looking cars than ours. She was humiliated to be seen in it. She didn't even want to acknowledge that the car belonged to us, because it was such an old heap. When she concluded that tirade, her father didn't say a word, didn't even respond, because it was true. We probably were driving the oldest car on that post.

So you see, she had some justification, but I couldn't let that go. I said, "Listen, Sugarpuss, if anybody wants to know why your dad is driving such an old and dilapidated looking car, I want you to smile. Because that is where the new car is—in your mouth!"

She didn't think that was very funny. I remember that she sashayed up the stairs in anger, grumbling about her mother and father. But we have lived long enough to receive a rather interesting epistle from this daughter. In this letter, she identified the many things for which she was grateful to us. Among them—at the top of the list, as a matter of fact—was "I'm so grateful that you would do without a new car so that I could have a Pepsodent toothpaste smile."

So hang in there. There will probably come a day when your child will recognize and identify the many sacrifices you made as evidence of your love for them.

But, as they are growing from little children on up to adolescence, the only way they really know you love them is if you tell them so, if you verbalize it, and demonstrate it.

IT ISN'T ALWAYS EASY TO
DEMONSTRATE OUR LOVE

One family had a fifteen-year-old son who would not allow his mother to hug or kiss him. The other five children happily accepted an affectionate hug or pat or quick kiss as they left for school. But not

Ron—he repeatedly pushed his mother away.

Finally his mother said to him, "Ron, we have to have some physical contact daily, but you may decide what it will be."

Ron asked, in absolute seriousness, "Could we shake hands?"

His mother agreed that would be fine. So, as he left for school, they would solemnly shake hands.

One day, after about a week of this, he said, "Okay Mom, Okay," and put his arms around her and gave her a quick kiss. She said she was so moved she could hardly keep the tears back, until she heard him say with satisfaction, "Well, that's one I can cross off."

"What do you mean?" the mother asked.

"The note, the note," he muttered as he handed it to her.

The note was one she had written him which said, "These are your chores. Do them today without fail. Empty the garbage, make your bed, clean your room, Love, Mother."

Sometimes, it is especially hard to be openly loving if you have a child who has some of your own personality traits. Have you found it more difficult to have a really loving, demonstrative relationship with a child who has some of your own character flaws?

Somehow we feel we have an absolute, moral responsibility to dig out those flaws, to make sure that we extricate them from that young person, regardless of what it takes. However, each child is, specifically and marvelously, a unique human being. That child was not meant to be an extension of you or of your ego. All children have been sent to us from a loving Father on high, and we have a responsibility to provide a loving, nurturing, accepting environment where they can grow up and fill the measure of their creation.

THE NEED FOR LOVE IN OUR LIVES NEVER CHANGES

We never outgrow our need for love, whatever our age. As a matter of fact, our need for love is so compelling that we spend our entire lives in search of it. Part of the reason for this is that we have a very poor ability to see ourselves. We cannot judge ourselves properly, and we do not understand ourselves fully. We look to others for understanding and for judgment. We look to others to hold up mirrors so that we can see ourselves reflected. We do not know our own worth and beauty until someone reflects them back to us.

I am reminded of the story of Lt. Col. Chaplain Claude Newby, U.S. Army, a convert to the Church and a highly decorated combat chaplain. He was raised in the hills of Tennessee. His family was certainly "poverty level." Claude was held back in grade school for two years because the school regarded him as retarded and unable to learn. However, Claude's mother defended "her boy." Every time the school suggested Claude was too slow for public school, she responded, "You don't see the light in his eyes because you won't take the time to *look*."

The event the students looked forward to the most each school year came when a bus was chartered to go to a distant town for a ball game. For one such occasion, Claude worked hard and collected enough whiskey bottles to sell to a moonshiner for the necessary one dollar bus fare. Before the trip, the principal came to Claude's class to take a head count of those students who would be going. He passed up and down each row, but when he came to Claude's desk he said, "No use asking—I know you aren't going." Claude was too humiliated to correct him.

Whatever his heartache or humiliation, Claude's mother would say simply, "Son, I believe in you." Claude's life began to change as his picture of himself began to change.

When Claude was in the seventh grade, a near riot broke out on the school bus. The huge bus driver stopped the bus, restored order, and threatened, "If there is one more word spoken, that student will be expelled from school." The bus was deadly quiet until the bus began to move again. Then, despite the warning, a student sitting next to Claude began to talk. Claude had not uttered a word. The bus driver accused Claude of talking, and amidst the jeers of the other students, put him bodily off the bus, saying he could not return to school unless his father personally brought him to the principal.

At home that night, when Claude told his story, his mother stood up and said, "I believe you son." His father, influenced by her firm belief could not protest. The next day this mountaineer father, grim-lipped, took Claude back to school. The principal heard Claude's story and said quietly but with conviction, "I believe you, too, Claude Newby. Your mother has raised you right."

Though she was old beyond her years, worn and tired from her tasks as a mother of many children, though she had no education and no personal opportunities, she took the time to see the light in her boy's eyes when others saw him only as slow.

This mother, who had never been to school, said, "I believe in you," and when a judgment was to be made she said, "I believe *you.*"

Claude Newby, whom the school had seen as retarded, went on to receive advanced degrees, and he encouraged others to do the same. While in the service, he saved lives and affected many others positively. Who can estimate his personal impact in a thirty-year military career?

How and why did this happen? Because he had a mother, who, although she could neither read nor write, *loved* him and *believed* in him. When a mother can do that, it matters little what else she can or cannot do.

Parents are those first, most important people who care for us, warm, nurture, and love us and speak to us in a kind, loving way. Those first nurturers become almost gods to us, because they have absolute power over our life and death. We are dependent on them for our food, our warmth, and our care. We reach out in a primeval way to them.

But as the scenario changes, we sometimes move away from our parents. In this process, I have observed that those of us most difficult to love, most abrasive, need love the most. It should be a rule of thumb that when you have a child who irritates you to the extreme—who is abrasive and rubs you the wrong way—that child, as a general rule, is identifying for you, not so much how he feels about you, but more importantly, how he feels about himself.

Arrogant, hard to manage, mouthy children that wound our egos by their rebuffs, need in a very large measure, our continuing verbalization of love and appreciation and our hanging in there with them. Hang in there to let them know how deeply you care. Let them know, that though certain behaviors may be unacceptable to you, and disciplinary steps must be taken, there isn't anything they can do that would cause you to stop loving them. Every child needs to know that you would love him, seek for him, go wherever it is necessary to go, because you love him.

UNCONDITIONAL LOVE

As the scenario changes in your parenting, and that little baby, so easy to love, so easy to embrace, so easy to praise, becomes not so easy to love, and embrace and praise, keep in mind that, in direct proportion to his cantankerousness, he needs your appreciation and love and approval of him as a human being.

I do not mean by an accepting environment that we need to accept behavior that is not good or wise or moral. I believe in discipline.

Discipline is a reality of life. Our children must be taught a healthy respect for discipline. If it is not taught in the home, if children are not taught to understand that this is a part of life, we have done them a great disservice. But discipline implies love.

The hardest thing we have to do as parents is to be able to separate the actions from the children who perform them. Regardless of what children do, they need to know there are people in their life who will always love them unconditionally.

We receive that kind of love from our Heavenly Father. If we felt our Father in Heaven's love was a conditional love, life would be devastating for us. In other words, if we felt our Father in Heaven might say, at any time during the course of this life, "I've had it with you. I've tried to be patient and understanding, but this is the end. This is the absolute end. Depart hence from me," life would be unbearable. If we thought we would ever arrive at the point with our Father where he would never again hear our pleas for forgiveness nor understand our need for him, wouldn't it be devastating? Yet, without unconditional love, this fear could be realized, and unless we communicate unconditional love to our children, they may fear such abandonment from us.

It is hardest to show unconditional love when a child is totally different from us or does not live up to our expectations. Many years ago, in a class at the University of Maryland, Dr. Gesell addressed this problem. He held up his outstretched hand and said, "If there are five children in a family, the children are usually very similar—some shorter, thinner, etc.—but like these fingers, very much alike. However, in most families there is a thumb. Parents moan about the thumb. What have we ever done to deserve a thumb? Don't moan," said Dr. Gesell. For thumbs, as odd and different and even unrelated as they may seem, usually turn out to be very worthwhile human beings.

By exercising unconditional love, we can recognize and accept the uniqueness of each of God's children.

IS ANGER THE OBSTACLE?

Why don't we express our love more often and demonstrate our caring? Is it because of anger? Is that one of your parental weaknesses? Do we rationalize that we are justified in our anger and that we would not be angry if our children would obey us or if they were not so difficult? President Kimball stated that self-justification is the greatest sin, for it is the father of all other sins. We must be careful that we do not justify our anger. It is not the events or the children that lead us to angry outburst, but our own lack of self-control and habits of response to events and people.

I remember a story a woman once told me about a red blouse. She said her teenage daughter had asked for a particular red blouse for Christmas. In fact, the daughter would not let it go, even though her mother told her the blouse was too expensive. The daughter cajoled, whined, and begged, until finally the mother decided that since her daughter wanted it so badly, she would sacrifice and find a way to purchase the red blouse. On Christmas morning, when the daughter opened the package and tried the blouse on, she was disdainful and decided she didn't like it after all.

This mother experienced such feelings of anger toward her daughter that she felt her Christmas was ruined. She went into her bedroom and knelt down and asked Heavenly Father to help her so she wouldn't ruin everyone else's Christmas. As she knelt there, a sweet peace came over her, and in her mind she heard these words, "This has given you a chance to develop Christlike love. Be grateful, not resentful."

As I talked with this woman later, I pointed out that I was sure Christ would feel that same anger toward us at times if he were not the perfect being that he is. Our carelessness and ingratitude toward the gift which he has given us could evoke his anger, but he loves us unconditionally even if we do not accept his gift with gratitude.

As parents, we must prayerfully gain the strength to be able to love our children unconditionally, as Christ loves us, and to overcome our own tendency toward anger. I believe we were given the parenting experience to help us develop love and self-mastery. Parenthood is a wonderful training ground for developing those qualities.

WHAT WILL YOUR CHILDREN REMEMBER?

Your children will not remember how clean the house was or the things you bought them, but they will remember the feelings that evidenced your love.

As our children assembled together recently for a Christmas get-together, we asked them to recall for us the memories of holidays past. Not a single one of them spoke of a gift, but what they recalled were feelings. These are the things that live forever, but they are not necessarily self-generating. We have to take the time to make sure that we are creating an accepting atmosphere in our home and that there is plenty of "show and tell" time when we demonstrate our love.

In summary, let me quote from a letter I received from a mother who attended an Education Week class I taught at BYU:

> You challenged us, as mothers, to find an area where we could excel. I prayerfully selected the one thing I wanted to become an expert in. I decided that with five precious, active children, this was the ideal time to try to become an expert in motherhood. (My! That is a presumptuous and scary statement to see in writing, but nevertheless that was my decision!)
>
> I decided to use the standard works as my texts, the Lord as my counselor, and my priesthood holder husband as my partner and advisor. The first test was not long in coming.
>
> Our nine-year-old son, the only male of our five children, wrote a terrible note at school, which expressed things I never dreamed he would ever think about. The note was diverted from its destination by an alert third-grade teacher, and I got the word from her. Of course, I was shattered.
>
> Here I was without my husband to help because he is an airline pilot and was out of town. I was alone, and my only son needed a good father-son chat, and I was feeling inadequate to the challenge.
>
> First, I sent the culprit to his room while I dealt with his sisters and got things under control, so I could go up and talk with him privately.
>
> As I mounted the stairs to go to his room, I was really frightened. What on earth could I say? Fortunately, I had to pass my own room on the way to his. Quickly I went in, closed the door, knelt down and asked the Lord to use me however he needed in helping this precious boy, our son and his.
>
> I entered that boy's room still not knowing what to say. I sat and waited for the words to come. But the Lord didn't bring words, he brought tears—mine and then my son's. Only then the words came, and I explained how degraded I felt, and how I felt like I had failed as a mother. Then I knelt and told the Lord the same things.
>
> Now came that dear boy's response. He was in tears, and he put his arms around me, sobbing out his love for me. He

said he was sorry, and then he, too, prayed. He told the Lord he loved me and wanted to honor me, and he promised he would never do those things again.

We spent a long time with our arms around each other expressing our love and getting control of our emotions. It took all I had in me to follow the Lord's direction, and I felt totally drained after this experience, but it was worth it!

I am certainly not an excellent mother yet, but from this experience I know the Lord can help me step by step if I can stay in tune and listen and follow his directions.

That, my dear friends, is the secret of good parenting. Try to get in tune, and give yourself credit for any little step of progress you are able to make in that direction.

My message to mothers is always the same. Don't beat yourself up because you feel you are a lousy parent. Don't get caught up with "I should have" or "I ought to." You are probably a better mother than you think.

THE TRUE MASTERPIECE

A mother of four preschool children, a gifted art major who married a year before she would have graduated, related a lesson she learned about the Lord's perspective of motherhood. She was going through a hard time and felt that the walls of her home were closing in on her. She needed to get out of the house and go someplace to relax and rejuvenate, but her husband wanted to stay home. She was invited to accompany her parents to visit her aunt and uncle in San Francisco, and her husband suggested she take their four-month-old baby and accept their offer. He offered to care for the other three children. She was elated.

While she was in San Francisco, she visited several art galleries. The show that captured her the most was devoted to the art of stained glass, which had been her specialty in college. She stood enraptured before one window which was being displayed in such a way that the sunlight set it ablaze with life and color. She stood there thinking, "I could be doing this kind of creative work. I *should* be doing this instead of struggling with these children." She suddenly felt hot tears coming to her eyes and in agony, she prayed, "Oh, Father, help me."

Her aunt was holding her four-month-old baby daughter, and in the quiet of the room, a beautifully dressed woman stopped to look at the baby, touched her cheek, and then in a voice for all to hear she said, "This baby is the true masterpiece in this room."

My young friend felt as if the Lord had spoken to her directly. With tears in her eyes, she said to me later, "I know what that woman said is true, and I know Father will provide the opportunity for me to do creative art forms later if I will appreciate the masterpieces I now have and what I must do while working in *this* art form."

YOUR BEST IS GOOD ENOUGH

A young mother in my stake recently died, leaving a family, the youngest member of which was ten years old. She was in her own home the last two weeks of her life and in those last sacred days, it was my privilege to talk to her. Do you know of what she spoke? Of her concern for her husband and children. She felt guilty because she was putting them through so much pain and anguish as she was dying. Her very last words were concern for their welfare, not for her own. She was dying of cancer and was in great pain, yet she did not want *them* to suffer. How ironic. She was a normal mother, impatient, sometimes angry, one who had regrets for nagging.

At her funeral, the stake president shared this young mother's feelings of being needed and of her importance to her family. She had told the stake president that if anyone at her funeral said she was needed beyond the veil more than she was needed here with her family, she would rise from her coffin and declare: "That is not true!"

Here was a mother (with a sense of humor) who had done the best she knew how, and her best was good enough. Despite what we mothers think and feel about ourselves, this is a good description of most mothers.

A mother is simply someone who does the best that she can with what she has to work with. Knowing that, you can have confidence in yourself and shed inappropriate guilt. Would the Lord condemn you for your failure to do what you didn't know how to do or didn't understand or didn't have the strength to do? Never.

Mothers, be comforted if you are putting forth your best efforts. Be at peace in your minds and in your hearts. In the sight of the Lord, your best is good enough. What else matters?

Section Three

Up Up and Away!

Positive Perspectives for Life

7
Happiness
Is a Choice

....

A HAPPY MAN

My husband bought me a new home in Texas just before he left for Viet Nam. It was my first, brand-new civilian home. My husband left it up to me to put in the yard. Landscaping became a back-breaking, disappointing task to me. I dreamed of what it would be like to have enough money to hire a landscape gardener to come in and do all of these things.

I fought the sand, wind, and weeds endlessly. One day, in despair, I telephoned the largest nursery in that part of Texas and ordered a hundred dollar's worth of flowering plants. That was a lot of money, and I really couldn't afford it, but I rationalized that those plants would make at least the front yard attractive.

I couldn't wait for the nursery truck to come. When it came, I ran to the door and there stood a Mexican-American man with one small box in his hand. I asked him, "What's this?"

He said, "Señora, it is your order."

I said, "My order?! Do you mean to say that those few scragglylooking plants in that pitiful little box are my order and they cost me a hundred dollars?"

He said, "Si, Señora."

That was the last straw. I'd been tired, worried, and despairing, and I sat down on the front steps and began to cry. Men often find a woman's tears most disconcerting, and this fine man was no different. He patted my shoulder awkwardly and said, "Señora, please, Señora do not cry."

Of course, the more he said, "Señora, don't cry," the more the Señora cried. Finally, he said, "Señora, please let me talk to you." He sat down beside me and began to speak. His name was Juan Garcia. He'd been born in Mexico, but the dream of his life had just been realized, and he was now an American citizen. He asked me if I understood how wonderful it was to be an American citizen and if I understood how wonderful this land was. He told me how much he loved the land. "Señora," he said, "the earth, the land, she is alive, she is good, and she will serve us all if we but love her. You need to know only a few things, and then do these few things with love, Señora."

He began to tell me the things I should do—what I ought to buy and ought not to buy, how to plant my plants, and how and when to fertilize and water them.

I have never known such a walking encyclopedia about plants. I learned other things about this great human being. His family was large, but his salary was small. He had few worldly possessions, but he was a happy man. There was joy evident in his good brown features. It was a contagious joy.

He spent a whole hour with me, and my spirits were lifted. He would not accept a single cent for what he had done. All he wanted was a drink of water. He had taken his lunch hour to give me all this advice free of charge, and he drove away happily eating a cold corn tortilla.

I felt better. I felt buoyed up. I no longer was in a pity party. I even felt richer. Do you know what I did with those feelings? I went to the telephone and called the nursery.

I insisted upon speaking to the owner of the nursery himself. When I got him on the phone he was very curt, really very crotchety, but I told him briefly exactly what had happened. I told him about my husband being in Viet Nam, that I had to put the yard in by myself, and that I was in despair and worried. Then I told him about his employee, Juan Garcia.

I concluded with these words: "Mr. Black, I am so impressed with the caliber of a company that would have as one of its employees a man as gracious and knowledgeable as Juan Garcia, that if I ever buy another plant, I'm going to buy it from Black's Nursery."

There was a silence on the other end. "Mr. Black? Mr. Black, are you still there?" In a moment, a quiet voice came back, no longer curt and surly. "Mrs. Johnson, I have been in this business for twenty-three years, and this is the first time anyone has ever said anything quite so nice. It means something to me. I thank you and God Bless."

As I hung up the telephone I thought, "What's wrong with Mr.

Black? In twenty-three years nobody's ever said anything that nice to him?" The conclusion I drew was that Mr. Black lived in a big home, drove a new car, had a prosperous business, and a lot of that green stuff called money. Probably, no one ever felt they needed to say anything nice to Mr. Black because it seemed that he already had everything. However, things do not guarantee happiness—happiness is a choice and an attitude, and has little to do with material objects, as this next story illustrates.

Once I was asked to come to a home—but it was not really a home but a sumptuous mansion owned by a family I knew. I had never been in one quite like it before. The bedroom to which I was ushered was larger than my own living room, and it had green Chinese rugs on the floor. A beautiful woman was lying on a bed that had a pale, green chiffon canopy over it. She was dressed in a dressing gown that must have cost a fortune, and she wore emeralds in her ears and on her hands. There was just one major flaw. She was dead by her own hand and had left a suicide note: "Dear David, I am sorry I had to do this to you, but there is nothing left for me to live for."

What a tragedy. This woman had "everything," according to the world's definition, yet in her mind she had nothing.

HAPPINESS: A CHOICE AND AN ATTITUDE

Happiness is a choice. It is not attached to material possessions, and it is not attached to power, position, or age. Happy people, regardless of their age, race, or socioeconomic background, do share some characteristics. For example, they seem to draw others to them. They do so because they are enthusiastic and find joy in life.

Happy people smile readily. Don't you love people who smile? Why don't we smile more? I hear clients say, "Why should I smile? I'm not happy." I say to them, "We don't smile because we are happy, we are happy because we smile." We generally wait for the feeling and then we act, but that's putting the cart before the horse. Do the thing, and the feeling will come.

Henry Fawcett was a distinguished member of the English Parliament. William Gladstone appointed him Postmaster General and he made great contributions to England in the fields of postal service and telegraphy.

Henry Fawcett was blind. The tragedy happened when he was twenty years old while hunting with his father. His father accidentally discharged his gun and hit his son in the face. The boy lived but was blind for the rest of his life.

His father wanted to kill himself, and young Henry wanted to die, too. He had lost hope. He thought he would never be able to read again nor return to school because he was unable to see.

One day he overheard his father crying and condemning himself for ruining his son's life. Henry decided right then that he had to help his father—at least bring some hope to his father, whom he loved dearly. He began to pretend. "Don't worry, Dad. I can go back to school. I'll have others read to me," he said. Outwardly, Henry began to live a life of optimism and enthusiasm but he admitted in his heart that it was all an act. He only pretended that his life had some purpose to keep his father from self-destruction.

But then something happened. There came a time when acting became reality. The game of pretense became truth. Hope grew in his heart, and hope produced great results. He had experienced the "as if" principle: act as if something is true, and it will become true.

We create in our minds the world in which we live. The world we create is a result of our thoughts and feelings. Our lives are composed of thoughts and feelings, not merely events. We have very little control over external events. We cannot control our spouse or our children (although we may try). We cannot control our in-laws or the neighbor's dog, or our boss. We cannot control world events, the weather, or the government.

But there *is* one thing we can control, and exercising that control is the only thing which can bring us peace. We can control our thoughts! Because our thoughts influence our feelings, control over our thoughts brings control over our feelings. When our thoughts are uplifting and positive, our feelings will be, too. When our thoughts are negative, our feelings will be pessimistic and depressed. The kind of world we create for ourselves, despite what is happening outside of us, depends on the thoughts we choose.

WHAT WE CAN LEARN
FROM THE "HAPPY FISH"

I love porpoises and dolphins. It gives me a lift every time I see them. They seem to be such joyful creatures. Their mouths turn up in such a delightful smile.

We've learned some rather tremendous things about porpoises

and dolphins in the last twenty years. They have a high degree of intelligence, and an instinct and power for good that is overwhelming.

There are many stories of people whose lives have been saved by dolphins. One reason for this may be the natural response of the female after she gives birth to her baby under water. (I realize that dolphins are actually mammals and not fish!) The first act she performs, following birth, is critical. The mother must lift the newly-born dolphin to the surface for its first breath. If she does not, the baby dolphin will die.

So powerful and loving is this female instinct that when she sees other struggling animals or humans in the water, she will buoy them up to the surface instinctively.

Happy people, giving and nurturing people, seem to have a similar ability to buoy up others, to bring them to the surface when they are sinking in the problems of life.

I have clients say to me, "Lucile, I know what you're talking about, I hear this all the time, but it's just not my nature to be that way. I'm naturally pessimistic. I'm a natural worrier and a downer. That is an inherited quality. All my people are like that. I don't see anything I can do about it."

I quote to them from Stephenson, "I am not responsible for the kind of a disposition I brought into this world, but I am responsible for the kind of a disposition I take out of this world."

LEARNING TO MAKE HAPPY DECISIONS

Someone once asked me, "Do you think you have the right to tell people how they can be happy?"

I replied, "Not really. The only thing I can do is to share correct principles and contrasting principles and let people connect those principles with their own thinking and behavior. Hopefully, through this process, they can become empowered to make wise happiness-producing decisions."

Our personal fulfillment and happiness are connected to our ever-increasing enlightenment. Once insight is gained and connections are made between principles and personal behavior, then people gain the knowledge which can free them from dysfunctional patterns.

Why do people often fail to free themselves from dysfunctional behavior even after they have obtained the knowledge required to change? What is the problem? It is often pride. The principle, "Ask, and ye shall receive," is a true principle but it involves ridding ourselves of pride and having the humility to ask for help. The contrasting principle is also true: "If ye do not ask, ye shall not receive."

OVERCOMING THE "FATAL FLAW"

The Greeks have taught, through their drama and literature, that people often have a tragic flaw. They identify that fatal flaw as pride. The Greeks believe that mankind, of their own volition, by the very nature of their mortality, tend to assume that they are invincible and that they can solve all their own problems. The Greeks call this assumption of self-sufficiency a fatal flaw. Throughout the scriptures, both ancient and modern, we are cautioned against this same flaw of self-sufficiency and pride.

A young man who lives in northern Virginia had caused a lot of pain by his behavior, activities, and addictions—not only for his family but for himself. Then his sister, whom he loved very dearly, was discovered to have a pernicious kidney disease. She needed a kidney transplant. Doctors determined that out of all the possible donors, Robert's kidney would be the best match. Robert agreed to donate his kidney to his sister, Ruth, but with stipulations. He said to her, "What guarantee do I have you will take care of my kidney? You have always been careless with your own health. What if I give you my kidney and you throw my kidney away? What promise do I have that you will honor this gift?"

I was very interested in what his father, the stake president in that area, had to say to Robert regarding the gift of his kidney. He said, "When the Lord Jesus Christ's body was racked with pain and torment, and blood ran from every pore as he willingly paid the price that justice demanded for our personal sins and corruption, He extracted no promise from you, Robert, that unless you honored his gift of victory over the grave, you would not benefit from his gift of salvation from death and hell. It was a gift he freely gave to all, and there were no strings attached. It was not based on your worthiness, it was based on unconditional love, and that's what you must do with your gift to your sister. It must be presented and given freely as a gift of love."

Robert agreed, and a remarkable thing happened as a result of his gift freely given. None of the treatment centers, none of the other things that had been tried as Robert stumbled and fell and stumbled and fell had helped. But the giving of that kidney has done more for this young man to face him in the proper direction, and to incline his ears to hear the counsel of our Father, than any other event in his life—because it involved overcoming his pride.

HAPPINESS IS SOMETIMES MEASURED IN TEASPOONS

My husband's sister suffered a stroke some years ago which left her paralyzed on one side. Rhea and her husband, Clifford, had had a great, and even an exciting, marriage. He was a handsome Air Force flyer, and she was a gifted and beautiful musician. However, he was not a member of the Church and felt no need for God in his life. All of the extended family loved him, but we had no idea of the spiritual giant that was sleeping within him until this tragedy.

After months of hospitalization, Rhea came home, and Clifford retired from his job to assume her full care. It was not easy. Because she was unable to do anything for herself, caring for her turned into an awesome labor of love and a never-ending list of duties for Cliff.

He could have said, "This is more than I can do, and I need to put her in a nursing home," and he would have been justified. But, instead, each time a family member visited, we saw a cheerful, even grateful, couple. They were not merely gritting their teeth and enduring. There was good will, good humor, and even joy evident in their relationship as these two friends came to grips with their tragedy.

Our whole family attended Clifford's baptism. Instead of the tragic circumstances of his life embittering him, it had stretched his soul, helped him understand the purpose of life, and opened his heart to truth. His selfless service to Rhea made of him a new man, and the spiritual sleeping giant within him awakened.

I asked Clifford to write me a list of things he and Rhea had done the past six years since the stroke to find happiness. He said, "What did we do? Happiness is to be measured in teaspoons, not by great events like going to Hawaii. If we are on the alert, there are teaspoons of joy to be savored and enjoyed daily. We found them and enjoyed them."

ENJOY THIS MOMENT

The real joy in marriage, and in life, is to live in the now. Live in this day, this hour, this moment. We never know what will come tomorrow.

Happiness is a choice. As Abraham Lincoln said, we are usually about as happy as we make up our minds to be. When we are unhappy, we usually think it is because we don't have enough money, our house isn't big enough, we don't have a new car, or we wish we were at a different stage of life. And yet, how much money is the perfect amount? What is the perfect house, or the perfect car, or the perfect age?

If we fantasize that, somehow, someplace, sometime, we will have the affluence and perfect circumstances that will make us happy, then we are fooling ourselves. If we constantly live for the future, there will come a day when we will discover we have missed the joy that could have been ours all along the way.

MATERIALISM VERSUS HAPPINESS

This generation wants it all, and they want it immediately. Today, even the very young are concerned about wearing clothes with the right label. Many people are concerned about driving the right cars, owning a new home fully furnished with the right brands, and vacationing at the "in" places, whether they can afford it or not.

This mind-set leads to a desire for more and more. It leads to the habit of accumulating things, which can complicate our lives. When we have "everything," we need places to put it all! Our closets are often running over. We buy houses with two and three car garages and then leave our cars outside because the garages are already full. Storage units are greatly in demand. Pickups and vans are popular because we must have bigger vehicles to carry all our possessions.

But has affluence produced happier people? It would seem that the opposite may be true. If abundance brings happiness, we would assume people who have the most possessions would have the most happiness. Yet all the experiences of my life lead me to believe that the only reason there are more unhappy poor people than rich people is because there are so many more poor people than rich people!

As a young married woman, I would visit the quarters of senior fieldgrade officers' wives. Everything would be so clean and orderly. Sometimes, they would have Persian rugs on the floor, or all these marvelous pieces of Dresden and Meissen they had collected from all over the world. On the other hand, I had things in *my* quarters that had come from the Goodwill.

The officer's wife would come sweeping into the room in such luxurious elegance, with her nails and her hair freshly done.

I would think about my own hands with the nails broken, and the baby's spit-up all down my back because I had forgotten to burp him after breast-feeding him. I would sit there and wish that I could smell lovely and look lovely and have a home like theirs.

But I soon learned that many of these women were envious of me for my beautiful family and my good husband. I learned that I must not spend my time wishing my life away. Today, I have many nice things and my home is neat and tidy, but I am reminded of these words from the song "Sunrise, Sunset," "Where is the little boy I carried? Where is that little girl at play? I don't remember growing older, when did they?" I realize that my years of raising children was a very special time in my life, but so is this time in my life.

Choose to be happy with your present circumstances. Don't fantasize about when you will have a newer car or a better job. Don't spend your life wishing for the time when you will live in that beautiful home, complete with Persian rugs and Dresden. In Hebrews, the Lord tells us to be content with our present circumstances:

> Let your conversations be without covetousness; and be content with such things as ye have: for he hath said, I will never leave thee, nor forsake thee. (Heb. 13:5)

In the accumulation of things, people are really searching for contentment. What do we need in order to feel contentment? Paul tells us in 1 Timothy that food and clothing are all we need:

> But godliness with contentment is great gain. For we brought nothing into the world, and it is certain we can take nothing out of it. And having food and raiment let us be therewith content. (1 Tim. 6:6–8)

Not many of us would agree with Paul. But, maybe we could all agree that the secret of contentment is not in having much, but in wanting little. The first part of the scripture is the key—godliness with contentment. It is foolish to seek contentment through abundance because, as Paul says, we brought nothing into the world and we can take nothing out of it. Job also said it well: "Naked I came out of my mother's womb, and naked shall I return" (Job 1:21).

All we take out of this world is ourselves. However, with that self can go three powerful gifts: testimony, knowledge, and relationships.

Does that tell us where we should put our priorities in this life? Paul in Philippians said of himself,

> I have learned, in whatsoever state I am, therewith to be content. I know both how to be abased, and I know how to abound. . . . I can do all things through Christ which strentheneth me. (Philip. 4:11–13)

Jesus knows our gullibility and tendency to be enslaved by material things, and so he warns, "Take heed, and beware of covetousness: for a man's life consisteth not in the abundance of the things which he possesseth" (Luke 12:15). Jesus wants us to master our desire for things and not be manipulated by our desires for material wealth. The menace of materialism can be seen in what it does to our souls.

Materialism caused ancient Israel, though recently delivered from bondage, to want to return to Egypt and slavery simply for material comforts. Materialism is a faulty attitude about the things of this world. It is the spirit of "getting" rather than "giving." Materialism engenders greed and selfishness through self-indulgence. It is a personal choice to serve mammon rather than God. It is trusting our wealth to solve our problems and give us security, rather than turning to God, the only true and lasting source of security.

God does not condemn anyone for being prosperous, for owning property, or for being a financial success, but he gives us adequate warnings that these do not, in themselves, bring about peace or contentment.

ACCEPTING DIFFICULTIES AS PART OF LIFE

A man I will call John was in a blue mood, and he admitted it had to do with the time of the year. Labor Day weekend was coming up, and it was the last holiday of the summer and evoked unhappy realities to him with the shorter days. The children returning to school meant that he would have to attend all their sports and school activities. Also, his firm was busier in the fall. He admitted to feeling trapped when all his free time seemed to evaporate.

Speaking to me, John said he thought that my life—so different from his since my family was all raised—looked pretty easy, at least from where he sat.

I replied, "You are so wrong!" I told John a bit about my life. I was a bride in Alaska when World War II erupted. Our ship, full of military dependents, sailed under military escort for Seattle. Military Intelligence assumed the Japanese would now invade Alaska after bombing Pearl Harbor.

I didn't see my young husband for over two years—living with the constant fear I would never see him again. A baby daughter was born whom he never saw until she was nearly two years old. His war-time duty took him over seas again, this time to the worst Pacific battlefield. A baby boy was born whom he would not see until the baby was a year old.

The television kept me alert to the invasion of Okinawa. My husband landed with the initial beachhead. The invasion of Okinawa stands as one of the most brutal of all battlegrounds in the Pacific. I lived with the distinct possibility my husband's name would appear on the casualty list.

Those years of worry and sacrifice have forever impacted my life. He wore many medals, but they would not be the last ones. He fought in Korea. He fought in Viet Nam. It was a repeat of those early years. This time two purple hearts decorated his uniform when he returned home.

For those early years I was primarily alone raising our children. How did I survive? Because I thought—we thought—there were more important things than expecting life to be a rose garden. We believed in the principle of liberty. We believed in the principles of duty, honor, and country and knew these exact price. We continue to believe in these principles.

I told John, "So you think when children are grown and gone, all of your problems and trials go with them? Some of life's greatest trials come when married children, and grandchildren, experience heartbreak, trial, illness, and death. As elderly parents, you are still in the arena, only with less health and vitality to cope. Trials do not end. Growth and pain continue because there is purpose in pain."

Other people's lives may look easy, but that is only because we do not know all the circumstances of their lives and feelings of their hearts.

Difficulties are common in everyone's life. We should not believe that some people go through life like a breeze, and that nothing ever goes wrong for them. Life is hard for everyone. The particulars may be different for each of us, but the reality of personal struggle applies to all.

STRUGGLE: THE PRICE OF GROWTH

Brother Truman Madsen has said that there is no growth of soul, there is no development of spirit, there is no character growth except through stress and struggle and distress. That is the gospel and there is no other way. He indicated that God himself does not have the power to take away the ignorant and undeveloped self and make it into a God. Only through stress and struggle can that person grow to be a god.

Growth comes because we have been willing to pay the price of prayer and effort and sacrifice. In his celebrated book *The Road Less Traveled*, Scott Peck said, "Life is difficult. This is a great truth, one of the greatest truths. It is a great truth because once we truly see this truth, we transcend it. Once we truly know that life is difficult—once we truly understand and accept it—then life is no longer difficult—because once it is accepted, the fact that life is difficult no longer matters."

Until we accept the difficulty of life, we moan and groan about the enormity of our problems, kick against the pricks, pound on the vault door, or jump up and down to escape the truth, imagining that somehow, somewhere else, life is easy for others, and we have been cheated. What makes us think that life *should* be easy? When we really understand that we are not alone—that all others also experience trauma and hurts and problems just as we do—this perspective removes our sense of isolation.

Our personal growth and development, our increased spirituality, or our improvement in relationships all have different kinds of price tags. They do not come free. We do not always respond to difficulties and challenges in ways that help us grow. Depression is one response that is not growth-producing.

DEPRESSION: THE GREAT MIRTH-STEALER

Shakespeare's Hamlet bemoaned, "I have of late—but wherefore I know not—lost all my mirth." He was in a state of depression. This unpleasant state can be triggered by minor or major upsets in our lives. Even minor upsets, such as a friend not returning a call or a bad permanent, can cause us to feel depressed. There are also holiday blues and other blues caused by the seasons, the weather, and their relation to past memories. The blues may be a plain case of exhaustion—being a friend to everybody else but an enemy to ourselves. Serious depression may be triggered by major upsets in our life, such as divorce or the death of a loved one.

I asked my client, John, to write down the things he had told me about how he was feeling, and as he did so, he was astonished to realize he had felt this same way every Labor Day weekend he could remember. As a boy, his summers were carefree. He fished and roamed with his dog.

Then, after Labor Day, school began, there was the school bus to catch each morning, homework to do, crabby teachers, and at-home chores. He hated it. Therefore, Labor Day became the most depressing weekend of the whole year. As a teenager, he would stay in his room and sulk. But as a husband and father, he couldn't hide, so he took out his depression on his wife and kids—harping, dumping anger and criticism, complaining, blaming. He was miserable and made sure everyone else was, too.

ANCHORS TO THE PAST

In writing down what he was feeling, he was discovering anchors. Anchors are those situations, persons, or things which trigger memories of past experiences, thoughts and emotions. John had powerful negative emotions (or anchors) about Labor Day over the years.

Anchors tie a person in the here and now to feelings rooted in the past. Obviously, there are positive as well as negative anchors. Negative anchors can be changed by positive ones if the negative and positive are laid side by side. This is done by getting in touch with the negative memories and feelings—explaining them, talking about them—while, at the same time, building in new and happier experiences.

Since past experiences and the emotions we have about them are often anchored in holidays, seasons, or events, only new experiences and new emotions can replace the old ones.

TECHNIQUES FOR HEALING

There are therapeutic techniques that professional therapists use to help individuals replace negatives with positives, such as healing memories and visualizations. I often suggest writing down any negative feelings you can pinpoint and then trying to identify any "thinking errors" you may be making that may be contributing to those feelings.

Whenever you feel anxious, unhappy, confused, or resentful, ask yourself, "What am I believing now that may not be true?" Your negative self believes a lot of lies. I hear things like, "Life has not been fair to me," "I can never forget what has happened," or "I can never forgive those who wronged me. They have damaged me and changed me forever." None of these statements are true unless we make them true. This kind of thinking error allows us to hide behind self-pity.

I also hear statements such as, "I am a hopeless failure," or "I am a

mess—if only I could just get my act together, my life would be better."
These lies tell us we are victims instead of free agents. They allow us to
see ourselves like flies caught in spider webs. From that point of view, we
cannot see truth or understand the principle that we are responsible for
our choices and our lives.

One of the most effective techniques you can use to discover your
thinking errors is to improve your prayer life. Be consistent and honest
with Heavenly Father. Tell him what is really in your heart—your anx-
ieties, your hurts, your bruising memories—and then ask for healing.
Hebrews 4:13 tells us, "All things are naked and opened unto the eyes of
him with whom we have to do."

Heavenly Father already knows all your hurts, so bare your heart to
Him. Tell him exactly how you feel and why you feel that way. In
Exodus we see an example of Moses, who was certainly depressed, baring
his heart to the Lord. Moses said,

> Lord, wherefore has thou so evil entreated this people? why is
> it thou has sent for me? For since I came to Pharaoh to
> speak in thy name, he hath done evil to this people: neither
> hast thou delivered thy people at all. (Ex. 5:22–23)

Those were honest feelings and Moses needed help. He got that help, but
in the Lord's own timing, which is always perfect. The Lord will hear
your prayers and answer them in his own way and own time.

One other thing to be aware of—don't tell yourself you are okay
when you are not. Admit to yourself, emotionally, the truth about your
life. Dump the negative garbage out! I tell people to create a "Mad Book"
by writing out their negative emotions and feelings so they can look at
them and then get rid of them, tear them up, and throw them away.

I want to tell you about Rick. He was depressed due to guilt over his
behavior toward his mother. She had been obnoxious to him but now
was dead. He wanted me to make him feel better by helping him in his
self-justification, but to do that would have short-changed Rick.

Rick can't change the past. He can't change his mother's death, but
he can change his interpretation of the past. How? By stopping the
resentment he feels toward his mother, and by refusing to continue feeling sorry for himself.

I told him if he would abandon the victim profile that has filled him
with hostility, fear, and loneliness, then the past would no longer exercise this negative influence in his life. This is a great principle to dis-

cover—that when we are able to take charge of our feelings, the past itself will change for us! It is a true principle.

MAKE CHRIST YOUR WINGS

A young man, who had experienced great trial and loss, was a volunteer counselor for an encounter group. The room was filled with people in different stages of depression, and I was there as an observer. This young man stood up and said, "I want to tell you a true story about an eagle. If any of you have been on a Salmon River raft trip, you know how the river eventually begins churning with white rapids. On one of these trips, I saw, high on the cliff, a huge eagle. I watched as he soared and swooped down to the river to catch a fish, but this particular time he misjudged his speed and was caught by the rushing current. I saw the eagle bob up and down trying to rise above the water, but always being pulled back down. This beautiful, strong bird was sucked under by the current, and he disappeared from my view. I was so sad."

The people were nodding their heads sadly, and I could imagine them thinking, "Yes, that's me. I never dreamed this could happen to me, and I have been pulled under the water, and I can't swim, and I am going to drown."

"Wait a minute!" said the young volunteer counselor. "The story isn't over. Way down stream there was a churning commotion. It was the majestic eagle. It had broken free of the rushing torrent and was lifting off for the surrounding rocks. For a few minutes, that bedraggled bird rested on a rock in the sun, preening its soggy feathers. Then, it spread its enormous wings and rose higher and higher and was gone."

Then the young man said, "At times we feel sucked down into the depths of despair. Time after time, it seems we've gone under for good. But the Lord can hear our cries in the water and under the water, no matter where we are, and Christ makes it possible for us to be raised up out of hopelessness. He is our life jacket and our wings. He has the strength to help us rise above our circumstances, and we will!"

BOUNCE-BACK PEOPLE

I know some brittle people. Illness, disappointment, or bad luck can crack them into little pieces, like dried leaves, and they never recover.

I also know some people who can rebound or bounce back whole from a full-force hurricane of tough times. Such amazing personal resilience, or "bounce-backability", is a quality not all of us have developed, but it can often mean the difference between happiness and misery, life and death.

After my husband's near-death experience with a massive heart attack, we went to Hawaii for a month to encourage his recovery. Each day, we ate in the BYU-Hawaii cafeteria, and at lunchtime we would see an attractive woman, about fifty, tenderly caring for her husband who was seriously crippled. His body was misshapen, his hands curled under, his head and neck forced down nearly to his chest.

She fed him tenderly and carried on an animated conversation with him. He was evidently unable to speak but would nod his head. After several days, I approached her, introduced myself, and asked if she would tell me about her situation. She told me her husband had been a brilliant professor until struck down by this disease. I wanted to know how she could be so cheerful, because her cheerfulness was not a put-on, it was genuine.

She told me that she did not always feel so cheerful. She said, "When this tragedy struck, I almost shook my fist at the heavens saying 'This is not fair! What purpose can this tragedy serve?'" She said she felt guilty, tired, and angry all the time, until one day she hit bottom and concluded that death for them both would be better than the present situation. In her torment, she went to the scriptures, and in 2 Corinthians she read,

> Blessed be God, even the Father of our Lord Jesus Christ, the
> Father of mercies, and the God of all comfort; who comforteth
> us in all our tribulation, that we may be able to comfort
> them which are in any trouble. (2 Cor. 1:3–4)

She said, "This scripture went straight to my heart. It gave some sense, some purpose to my present situation." She started making what she called her "Glad Book," in which she recorded daily the small and simple ways the Lord comforted her. Then she began searching for ways she, in turn, could comfort her husband.

She found that the littlest things often made him the happiest—reading the comics to him, cutting out funny sayings for him, massaging his feet. She said, "All those things I can do sitting on the floor, so he can see my face." Picnics, popping corn, watching TV together, going for walks with him in his wheelchair with him pointing out, like a child, things he sees on the ground, and coming to this cafeteria are some of the ways they had found to bring happiness out of tragedy.

She said, "The students are so kind to him, and the faculty remembers him with love. I am no longer bitter. The Lord comforts me daily, so I can be a caregiver who has the privilege to comfort my dear husband. I have decided our Glad Book will be an important legacy for our family. As I reread some of my early entries, I am brought to tears remembering those sweet, fleeting impressions, those tender promptings that impacted my life daily when I needed help so badly."

Neal Maxwell talks about the pulpit of our memories and suggests that a spiritual experience is of little good if we have forgotten it. He encourages us to write them down, as this woman did. People who have "bounce-backability" seem to share the skill of keeping in touch with their spiritual experiences and good memories.

FINDING THE PATH TO HAPPINESS

Joseph Smith said,

Happiness is the object and design of our existence; and will be the end thereof, if we pursue the path that leads to it; and this path is virtue, uprightness, faithfulness, holiness, and keeping all the commandments of God. But we cannot keep all the commandments without first knowing them, and we cannot expect to know all, or more than we now know unless we comply with or keep those we have already received. (*History of the Church*, 5:134–35)

A dear sister from California who had experienced many heavy trials told me in a letter that she had become so discouraged that she often had to force herself to study and to pray. Her letter concluded with these words: "Each day as I continued to struggle in my pain, I became aware that at some time during each day the Spirit would give me a 'hug.' This fortified me so that I was equal to the tasks at hand." Think what an entry that would make in her journal to share with her posterity!

Bounce-back people choose righteousness. They focus on the good and the beautiful in life. They write down their spiritual experiences to remind them of the Lord's goodness. They do not allow themselves to fall into the trap of bitterness or to wallow in their own "pity parties." They seek for peace. They choose to be happy.

George Q. Cannon said some powerful things about happiness and joy:

> I will tell you a rule by which you may know the Spirit of God from the spirit of evil. The Spirit of God always produces joy and satisfaction of mind. When you have that Spirit you are happy; when you have another spirit you are not happy. The spirit of doubt is the spirit of the evil one; it produces uneasiness and other feelings that interfere with happiness and peace.
>
> It is your privilege, and it ought to be your rule, my brethren and sisters, to always have peace and joy in your heart. When you wake in the morning and your spirits are disturbed, you may know there is some spirit or influence that is not right. You should never leave your bedchambers until you can get that calm, serene and happy influence that flows from the presence of the Spirit of God, and that is the fruit of the Spirit. So during the day you are apt to get disturbed, angry and irritated about something. You should stop, and not allow that influence to prevail or have place in your heart. (*Journal of Discourses*, 15:361)

The sister who felt the spirit give her a hug each day wrote me another letter in which she shared how she had to seek for peace each day. It was essential for her emotional, physical and spiritual health. In answer to a prayer, she was led to the scripture in D&C 59:23, "He who doeth the works of righteousness shall receive his reward, even peace in this world and eternal life in the world to come."

Bounce-back people share some of the following characteristics. They rejoice in the goodness and success of others (they feel joy and not envy); they share uplifting experiences with other people so that they, too, might be uplifted; they testify to the comfort and healing that come from the Holy Ghost, who is the Comforter; they understand that the ultimate power to overcome difficulties lies in their faith in the Lord Jesus Christ and in his love.

SOME THINGS NEVER CHANGE

When we lived in Heidelberg, Germany, I was the Advisor for Family Affairs to the Commander-in-Chief of the U. S. Army in Europe. This wonderful experience gave me many opportunities to address the problems of military families throughout Europe.

I had been invited to address the North Atlantic Council of Girl Scouts. They were to meet in Garmish, Germany. When the theme of this conference was announced, I was in the United States, and it wasn't until I arrived back in Garmish and was sitting on the stand ready to give my speech that I learned what the theme was. A large banner across the back of the ballroom proclaimed the conference theme, "A Growing Girl in a Changing World." I was dismayed, for I hadn't prepared to address that topic at all. As the program proceeded, all the other speakers hammered home that theme. Then the Commander himself introduced me, which was a signal honor. When he got up, he said, "It will be very interesting to hear my advisor address this subject, 'A Growing Girl in a Changing World,' when of course, this is one of the areas of her expertise."

This was not true, and I was horrified, absolutely horrified! I was almost sick to my stomach. I prayed mightily, but I was wishing the floor would open up and let me pass right down into oblivion.

As I walked slowly to the podium, I was in despair. I stood for a moment and looked up at that bold banner displaying the theme. And then something happened—that black and white banner changed, at least for my eyes. It now read, "There are some things in this world which never change." That was the perfect vehicle for the things I had prepared to address, and in joyous amazement, I bowed my head for just a second to thank a loving Father who had heard the desperate prayers of such a foolish daughter.

At the conclusion of my address the General arose, and with some emotion said, "Lucile, how could you have been so wise? How could you have been so perceptive as to have chosen to address the unspoken theme of this conference? For, of course, the unspoken theme—which is the most important part—is the need to abide the unchanging values in this life that are given to us by God."

I said, "General, I owe it all to a loving Father."

And the General said, "Well, Lucile, you must have some father!"

I assured him that, indeed, we do.

Indeed, we do have a wonderful Father who has allowed us to experience the principle of free agency in this life. Because we have our agency, we can choose to be miserable, or we can choose to be happy. Happiness is a choice! As for me, I choose to be happy!

~ 8 ~
A Forever
Brand of Beauty

Edgar A. Guest wrote some amusing lines that have a real message in them.

> Some folks in looks take so much pride,
> they don't think much of what's inside.
> Well, as for me, my face
> will ne'er be thought a thing of grace.
> So, I think I'll see what I can do for the inside of me,
> so folks will say, "He looks like sin,
> but ain't he beautiful within?"

All of us consider beauty to be an extraordinarily valuable commodity, but I'd like to consider what beauty really is. Thoreau said it this way, "We are all sculptors and painters and our material is our own flesh and blood, and our own bones. Any nobleness begins at once to refine a man's features and any meanness or sensuality to embrute them."

There is a saying that goes something like this, "At twenty you have the face you inherited, at forty you have the face you have developed and at sixty you have the face you deserve!

The far easterners have two expressions for beauty. *Maya* is everything on the outside—the wrapping, the package, which the Hindu religion teaches is only illusion. But they identify the more important of the two as "essence" or the beauty that is within, and I think they are right.

One of my favorite quotes is by Conrad Richter who refers to inner beauty in this way, "In the faces of women who are naturally serene and peaceful, and those rendered so by religion, there remains an 'after spring' and later an 'after summer'—the reflex of their most beautiful bloom."

THE MYTHS WE COMPARE OURSELVES TO

How is woman depicted by the mass media today? We are bombarded in this era by media pictures of beautiful women. Thanks to a lot of pure fantasy, and some feminist propaganda, today's woman is always described and shown as being gorgeous, exuding self-confidence, from the tip of her long lacquered nails to the top of her chicly coiffured hair, and she is often shown as being able to do anything a man can do and do it better. Of course, she always speaks as though she has a PhD in English, and she is always young, never ill, and never makes a mistake or appears foolish, never loses her cool, and never gains a pound. As a matter of fact, she is always seen as provocative and sensuous and perfectly put together. That woman is an absolute, total myth! If we compare ourselves to that kind of a woman, naturally we will come off feeling inferior.

There is a curious thing about this perennially gorgeous American woman, she has a curious inability to do anything traditionally feminine, such as cooking or sewing. Most importantly, she is almost never depicted as being a nurturing wife and mother, or mature in things of the spirit, and, as a result, most of us cannot identify with her.

On the other side of the spectrum, there is another woman we try to identify with. She is that perfect Relief Society sister—Molly Mormon. We see her at a Relief Society function, and her hair is perfectly done, and she wears clothes that are so chic. We fantasize about this woman. We think she must have her hair done in the most elegant salon, and she pays so much money for her clothes. But then, to our dismay, we learn she cuts her own hair, and the dress, that looked so chic and smart this morning, was actually a $2.95 remnant she whipped up last night. She is even more wonderful and resourceful than we had thought!

She has six children and wears a size 8 dress, and we think "It is absolutely not fair." Then she stands up and gives this wonderful Relief Society lesson, and you and I sit in the back of the Relief Society room and think, "I'll bet she left her house immaculate, and probably has dinner already made and in the fridge ready to warm up. Why can't I do that? I am a total loser. There isn't anything I do well, and if anybody could see my house the way I left it, they would probably call in the sanitation department, etc., etc." And, we leave Relief Society demoralized, dejected, and depressed. But I want you to know the woman we fantasize about is also a myth. We have concocted her in our heads, combining the strongest traits of many women into one.

You must not be guilty of comparing yourself with any other woman, because our Heavenly Father will not so judge you. He will ask only "What have you done with what you were given? Have you fulfilled the measure of your own creation?"

LOOKING WITHIN

A questionaire was sent to five-thousand middle-class, Christian women between the ages of twenty-seven and fifty to determine their greatest sources of depression. They were asked to pick the top three causes of their depression from a list of the following ten choices:

1. Absence of romantic love in your marriage.
2. In-law conflict.
3. Low self-esteem.
4. Problems with children.
5. Loneliness and boredom.
6. Financial difficulties.
7. Sexual problems.
8. Physical problems (health etc.).
9. Fatigue and pressure.
10. Aging.

To everyone's surprise, of those who responded eighty percent replied that their number one problem was *low self-esteem!* Yet, many of these women had degrees, were talented, capable women and many probably looked like Elizabeth Taylor did twenty-five years ago. Yet they admitted that low-self esteem was their number one problem! It would be an easy assumption, then, to say that most of us suffer from low self-esteem. If that is true for you, do you know from what your low self-esteem stems?

I have many women who say something like, "It's the way I look." They may say, "It's my large nose," or "my weight" or "the size of my bust," or whatever it is they don't like about their looks.

I am not underestimating the exterior at all. If you have the money, and you think that reshaping your nose will absolutely change your life, then go ahead and do it. But, be prepared that the surgeon will take an inordinate number of before and after pictures, because cosmetic surgeons have learned that patients may say after the operation, "You haven't changed me one bit." In other words, a nose-job will not necessarily change how you *see* yourself, because it does not change how you *feel* about yourself. So it would be with any other physical thing you could change.

Beauty, real beauty, as well as self-esteem, springs from within, and comes as a result of how we feel about life and about ourselves.

What you believe about yourself and about others paints itself on your face, colors your voice, and programs your thoughts, feelings, words and even your body movements. If you don't feel good and beautiful on the outside *and* on the inside, if you don't see yourself as a person of worth, and do not have positive self-acceptance, the sad fact is that rarely will anyone else see you as beautiful!

When you are immersed in negative thoughts about yourself, you broadcast a message in umpteen megacycles, "I feel inferior," (or worthless or self-conscious). These vibrations are picked up by others, and this influences not only how others treat you, but how you are able to treat them.

What you tell yourself and what you believe, is true for you, and you will behave accordingly. What you tell yourself and have faith in, is the greatest force in your life.

A NEW FORMULA FOR BEAUTY

I would like to give you a formula I have developed, and I say this: beauty equals T plus S to the 3rd power. The T stands for *tranquility*— a peaceful serenity. The first S stands for *spirituality*, the second stands for *self*, and the third for *service*. To me, beauty is a result of the tranquility we gain as we increase our spirituality, take care of ourselves, and reach out and serve others.

These are the areas over which we have absolute control, and over which we can actually do something.

If you agree with me that a woman who has that naturally serene and peaceful look truly is beautiful, it follows that if we would be beautiful, we must learn to reduce the tempo of our lives.

Beauty manifests itself as we get to the point that we make time for some quietness and time for reflection and study and meditation—when we take care of our inner life, which then allows us to be peaceful and serene in our daily walk with others.

William James, the great psychologist of this generation, said, "Neither the nature nor the amount of our work is accountable for the frequency or the severity of our breakdowns, but this cause lies rather in the absurd feelings of hurry, hurry, hurry and having no time, so that in breathlessness and tension and anxiety we live our lives."

Thoreau says, "Simplify, simplify, simplify." I can hear you say, "I hear you loudly, Lucile Johnson. No one in the world would like better to simplify their life. I would love to have some of that tranquility you speak about, and let someone else take over all of these little children, and the dirty dishes, and diapers, and dirty floors. I have even read Anne Morrow Lindberg's *Gift From the Sea*, and I could almost hear the breakers from that cottage on the beach, where Anne went. She was able to leave life's hectic tempo behind, and walk the shores early and late and collect seashells and write this marvelously tranquil book. Wouldn't I love to do that? However, diapers and dinner won't wait while I go to the seashore for six weeks.

You are right, all of the demands of your life are here and now. What do we do, then, as a result of the here and the now?

First, don't fantasize about that peaceful time in the future when the children are out of diapers and gone to school, or when the children are out of school and gone on missions. From my experience, the large increments of uninterrupted time for which you yearn, will never arrive.

Therefore, don't live in your thoughts out of the time you are in now. Your tranquility, your areas of time, must be here and now, and this formula is relevant, whatever your age or your stage in life.

Let me share with you some things I have learned in my busy lifetime. Perhaps, because you do not know me, you picture me as a woman who has not had your problems. I want to dispel that illusion. I have been married fifty some years and have five living children. I have followed a man in a green uniform around the world for thirty-five of those years. (After his retirement, he started following me!) I had to have my first baby without my husband present, and I had to take myself to the hospital. I had to have my second one alone and take myself to the hospital again. I've had children critically ill when he was overseas for so long in the wars. I have walked the floor worrying and weeping with exhaustion. I have gone through the very same problems with teenagers that many of you have today.

Those of you who are alone, I have been apart from my husband for forty-nine months except for brief interludes when he came home on leave or R&R. When a telephone rang in the middle of the night, the feeling would be so horrendous my heart would nearly stop with terror for fear I would hear from the other end, "Mrs. Johnson, this is the War Department. . . . We regret to inform you. . ."

I have lost my cool. I've been angry. I have shouted. I have felt I was the most horrible mother who ever lived, and really the most unloving and unnurturing wife. I want you to know that where you are, I have been too.

I have never had a time for long months by the sea, or at Walden Pond, or any of those other places you and I have wished to be. What I had to do was recognize that, perhaps, the demands will never cease, so I must not try to live out of the time I am in right now. I did not want to discover too late that I had missed the joy that was in the moment, or discover too late that many mundane things in my life held more pleasure than I was aware of at the time.

SPIRITUALITY

Where did I then reach for my tranquility? I reached into the area of spirituality. That brought me the greatest tranquility, and still does. I found, for my own self, arising early in the morning, before my companion was out of bed, and before my children were up, that in the quietness and peacefulness of my living room I could, on my knees, begin wearying our Father for my needs for that day. This brought me the peace I sought.

As I shared with him my worries and those things that stretched and pressed me, I learned he was my helper. I knew he would not provide for me an instant automatic maid/robot who would do all my tasks for me, but I learned he *would* provide for me remarkable and comforting things.

Matthew 11: 28–29 came alive for me as a young wife and mother, when I was inundated with more things than I felt I could do. Let me quote for you from the twenty-eighth verse, "Come unto me, all ye that labor and are heavy laden, and I will give you rest." Those words seemed directed to me, as I was burdened with mountains of diapers and washing and undone ironing. I believe those words were given for the weary wife and mother or the weary sister who is over her head in a job that is dissatisfying and stretches and presses her against her limits.

In the twenty-ninth verse, our Father goes on to say, "Take my yoke upon you, and learn of me." Now here is a key phrase, "*learn* of me; for I am meek and lowly in heart and ye shall find rest unto your souls." I found in my life, as I pled with my father to help me as I labored, I was able to perform those things I knew were my righteous tasks within my home and family.

I used to cry out in the mornings, and still do each day, "Oh God, are you there?" Then before I got off my knees each morning to begin whatever I had to do, alone or with little children, or with teenagers, or with my husband in the war, I would know that, whatever there was for me to do that day, I would be equal to it, and that sweet sense of peace—a warmth—would flood over me.

Then, I would open my scriptures. I am a convert to the church, and the Book of Mormon has been such an inspiring source of strength, and I have also discovered the Doctrine and Covenants is a marvelously inspiring scripture as well.

As I have read various revelations in the Doctrine and Covenants, I have taken the liberty of substituting my name in them, and they have thus taken on a more personal meaning. A great number of those revelations are pertinent and relevant to us today, whether we're up to our eyebrows in laundry that's not done or out in the marketplace earning a living.

Our primary source of spirituality, then, comes from prayer and scripture reading. The forty-sixth Psalm has been an inspiration to me. "Be still and know that I am God" (Ps. 46:10). As William James said, our lives are so filled with hurry, hurry, tension and anxiety, we feel we have no time. We cannot be beautiful on the outside, or on the inside, if that is the recipe under which we operate.

That is why I believe in taking the time in the quiet of the early morning hours, in the tranquility of our homes, to study and pray. It gives us a chance in that quiet, reverent atmosphere to reach out and know that Father's hand is there, that he is God. You will then begin your day able to feel a renewing of your spirit.

As you are scrambling eggs, or preparing the children for school, or your husband for work, or getting yourself ready for your work in the marketplace, you will then be truly ready for whatever will come that day.

The thirtieth chapter and fifteenth verse of Isaiah reads, "In quietness and in confidence shall be your strength."

Heavenly Father knows where you are at this moment. If you

would have the Lord with you all day long, seek him early in the morning. If you would keep him all day long, then reach out to him. Whenever you feel overwhelmed, whether you are on your knees scrubbing the floor, doing the laundry, or doing the dishes, communicate with him. One young sister said to me, "Sister Johnson, the only time I ever feel I have any quiet time alone with my Father in Heaven is when I can take my bath. I shut the bathroom door and lock it, and the children know at least when I'm in there, in the bathtub, I get to be there alone. That's when I carry on a conversation of all my yearnings and needs with my father." She said, "I hope he doesn't consider that disrespectful." He doesn't consider that disrespectful! Our Father knows that cleaning self, as well as cleaning bathrooms or cleaning clothes, is an important part of life and communicating with him is appropriate anywhere in your house.

There was a delightful letter in one of Ann Lander's columns from a woman in Nashville. She tells Ann, "One night I dreamed that I was walking along the beach with the Lord, and many scenes from my life flashed across the sky. In each scene, I noticed footprints in the sand. Sometimes, there were two sets of footprints. Other times, there was only one. This bothered me because I noted that during the low periods of my life, when I was suffering from anguish and sorrow, I could see only one set of footprints. So, I said to the Lord, 'You promised me, Lord, that if I followed you, you would walk with me always. But, I have noticed, that during the most trying periods of my life, there has been only one set of footprints in the sand. Why, when I have needed you most, have you not been there for me?' The Lord replied, 'The times when you have seen only one set of footprints, my child, is when I carried you.'" Yes, we are carried, we are buoyed, we are lifted and we are helped.

Our helper is not that maid we somehow fantasize will be produced for us, or some marvelous magical robot who could come in and do all of these mundane things. No, these are the things that we must do here and now and not be discontented while doing them. Father tells us in the scriptures that he will be our helper.

As you pursue your areas of spiritual growth and your spiritual stretching, I promise you your other pursuits of excellence, those things temporal, will come to you far more easily when you put first things first.

If we recognize tranquility as a source of beauty, and that the number one requirement for tranquility is spirituality, we will be on the road to real beauty.

SELF

There should never be more beautiful women in all of the world than you, who are members of the Church of Jesus Christ of Latter-day Saints, because of your knowledge. You know from where you come, and why you are here, and where you are going. That is extremely important knowledge. Knowledge is power. Each of us should stand like an exclamation point. Our shoulders should be back and our head held high. We should do the things that say to everyone within our sphere of influence, "She's such a beautiful woman."

The kind of beauty of which I am speaking doesn't have anything to do with the length of your nose, or the length of your eyelashes. This special kind of beauty I refer to is a beauty that comes with the self-confidence you have from within that you are a daughter of your Heavenly Father, and a daughter of a beautiful and magnificent celestial mother, in whose image you have been created. You have some real accountability to be responsible for yourself. You are the best visual aid the Church of Jesus Christ of Latter-day Saints will ever have. My premise here is that there is never enough beauty on the outside to compensate for the unbeautiful on the inside.

However, I am a practical therapist, and I know there are things we must each do to take care of the physical person. What are some practical things you can do that will enhance your outer self?

THE MAGIC OF DEEP BREATHING AND SMILING

One important, but simple, thing is learning how to breathe. Most of us are shallow breathers. When you are tense or angry or full of anxiety or inundated with mounds of work that has to be accomplished, watch yourself. The more anxious and tense you become, the more shallowly you breathe, and then your muscles become tense, and your body is tense, and that reflects in your face. If you have a baby, your baby picks up your tenseness, and he gets tense and fussy, and we wonder why it is always when we need him to be good that he acts the worst. Your companion and your older children also respond to your tenseness. So do the people who stand beside you in the grocery store, or sit beside you at church. You radiate vibrations. Our vibes very literally go out from us and identify for other people how we feel about ourselves and what we're feeling, and those vibes affect how others respond to us.

An exercise to relieve tension is to learn how to breathe. Get the oxygen up into your chest to oxygenate your face. Breathe deeply, and be a smiler, not a downer. No one likes to be around a downer, and a downer is not beautiful in anyone's eyes. Downers are people whose mouths turn down and their eyes turn down, their whole face seems to turn down. We have to fight the law of gravity all the time because it's constantly pulling everything we have down. The way to overcome the law of gravity, and the natural tendency to be grim and down in the mouth, is to be a smiler. A smiler is beautiful, and the world needs uppers. You have a tremendous ability to influence not only the people in your home, but all the people on the periphery of your life, when you smile. Have you noticed how children and babies respond to genuine smiles?

It has been said that some people are like sunshine, it is as if they have been plugged into the sun. The world beats a path to such people because they are a joy to be with and to look at. We need to be plugged into the sun.

MOVE THAT BODY

Another exercise for beauty is to move our bodies. When we feel blue and discouraged, when we feel down, and the dishes are just too much to do, or there are too many errands that have to be done, and too many children's demands, our inclination is to lie down on the sofa, and switch on the television. We rationalize it is to keep the children quiet.

That is a very poor exercise for beauty, either on the outside or the inside, and let me tell you why. Because, number one, it creates an appetite, and you can become hooked on television. You can become a television addict as simply as becoming addicted to chocolate, or anything else. Anything that creates an appetite for itself really is an addiction.

I find that often, my sweet, young, discouraged sisters use television as an escape from reality. When I talk to you, you say, "But Sister Johnson, I feel I'm not attractive. I am too heavy, and we're poor, and I don't have anything nice to wear, and the children are so difficult." You have a hundred absolutely bona fide things that make you feel down. But one of the major contributors to your list is unrealistic expectations placed on you by yourself or other people, or expectations caught from watching glamorized scenes on TV. So please be good to yourself and get rid of those unrealistic expectations.

Being good to yourself is not sitting in front of the television being cajoled into living in a fantasy world. Remember, everything you see on the television is a myth. Don't compare yourself to that chic woman on television who, with her painted nails, daintily puts that shirt with grease all over it into the washer, and two minutes later it is spotlessly clean. And, you can see this same woman's face in her shined linoleum. She's a myth. Don't get caught up in myths. You are living in a real world.

You be good to yourself. Being good to yourself is to get up off that sofa, even if you just have to pull yourself off. If your hair hasn't been brushed that day, get in there and brush your hair. Move, sisters, move! Soon you'll feel better.

Now you might say, "Oh, Sister Johnson, what are you talking about moving? That's my problem, I'm always moving, chasing toddlers or picking up toys or cleaning the house." I am not referring to that kind of monotonous moving. I mean moving with real vitality. Get outside, if you can, with the children.

If you can't get outside, try running through the rooms and playing a game with the children. You need your blood to begin to pump. That, in itself, is a beauty treatment.

I have a miniature trampoline I just love. I get out of bed every morning and get on it and spend at least thirty minutes there, and I get on it again in the evening.

For those of you who are joggers and can get out and jog or walk, remember to breathe deeply with your shoulders back, your head up like an exclamation point, and move. You will be amazed at the feeling of well-being you will have once you get yourself moving.

FOOD, GLORIOUS FOOD

If you were sitting in front of me, and came for counseling, I would say, "Tell me what you're eating." For the most part we, as women, are careless about what we eat. We're not careless about feeding anybody else in the family, but we are careless about ourselves. We feed our husbands and our children well, but we end up not having had time to eat, because we're sending our husband off to work, or we're sending our children off to school. Too often we become the food disposal for our family. We eat the soggy Cheerios and the sugared milk, or the scrap of toast.

You'll have more energy and more stamina, and your disposition will be better, if you will make sure you take time to eat nutritious meals.

Many of us become sugar-aholics. I speak from real experience. I am thinking especially of you with young children. At the end of the day when dinner has to be prepared, and your energy level is low, what do you reach for? You reach for something sweet, for a cookie or something easy. But don't. Reach instead for vegetables or a piece of fruit. Watch what you put inside your body, and be very, very careful of the amount of sugar you consume. It has been shown to have a great relationship to your personality, and how you feel about yourself.

BE AN EARLY-TO-BEDDER

Another thing you can do for yourself is to get enough sleep. I'm a great one for sleep. I used to be a night person, but I had to learn to change my clock when I had my children. Now, I am such a pro-early-to-bedder, early-to-riser. I would wish that all of us could get to bed and get at least an hour, to two hours, of sleep before midnight. I'm a firm believer in all that good sleep you can get before midnight. Then get up early in the morning.

When you can have that kind of rest you can get up in the morning and maybe get by for the rest of your life on seven hours of sleep. That would add ten to twelve years to your life in actual hours you could be up there producing and functioning.

GOOD GROOMING IS
WORTH THE TIME IT TAKES

It does take time, and effort, to make ourselves physically attractive. But you are a woman, a truly glorious human being. You owe it to yourself, and to your family, to be your most beautiful self.

Your hair needs regular care. Style, color, and curl are worthwhile investments and should be part of your budget. Your skin deserves nourishment, inside and out. Your nails should be well-shaped and clean. The clothing you wear should be appropriate, clean and attractive. Be good to yourself by considering the clothing you wear for your daily chores more important than the ball gown you may purchase for a very special occasion. Your everyday attire is how your most important audience, your family, sees you. Comfortable everyday attire is available now in such abundance and variation of prices there is no reason every woman cannot look clean, neat and attractive at any hour of the day, no matter what her activity.

Take the few minutes it requires each morning to put on your make-up, comb and curl your hair and dress appropriately. You will find that when you feel good about how you look this sets the stage for you to have a good, productive day, and to interact with others in a more positive way.

BE VITALLY ALIVE

Another way to be good to yourself is to be aware of the power of enthusiasm. Don't you like to be around people who are enthusiastic? Isn't it contagious? Enthusiasm comes from a word *entheos*, which means "God in you." It means being vitally alive and delighted to be alive. The gospel means good news, you have it all. You can reflect this when you are keeping things in perspective and trusting the Lord.

Your family will see themselves reflected in your enthusiasm. When you are up, and that's in many ways—up out of bed, and up with yourself, and standing like that exclamation point, and feeling good about yourself, and doing first things first—when that is a part of your lifestyle and you are literally up, you are like the tide. Then all the ships in the harbor rise—others in your home, and even on the periphery of your life, will rise to meet your enthusiasm for life.

For those of you who are not married, or are alone, you can also influence, in a great measure, other people where you work or live, by being up and positive and enthusiastic. We love to be around people like that. They send out sort of a positive life force, and so can you. If you've lost it for awhile, don't despair! The Lord will help you find it again. It is never gone, only buried for a time.

SERVICE

The third S stands for service. You might say, "Oh, Sister Johnson, I really wish I were able to expend large increments of time in service. But I don't have the time."

Let me tell you of one experience I had while in Canada for the BYU education circuit. Staying at a hotel one day, I called down to the dining room and asked that a chef's salad be delivered to my room.

Chef's salads sometimes are a ripoff. They have a couple of pieces of egg or pieces of cheese on the top and the bottom is all filled with greens. So I asked the woman in the kitchen, who took my order, "Is this a good chef's salad?"

And she said, "Oh yes, we make a very good chef's salad."

When the boy brought it to my room I looked at it very suspiciously, I was happy to discover it was a most delightful chef's salad. It had pieces of turkey and ham and eggs and cheese all through it. It was perfectly delicious.

As I was eating it and enjoying it, and carrying on a conversation with our Heavenly Father, which I sometimes do, sharing with him what a delightful salad it was, and how much I was enjoying it, he gave me to know I should let the person who made it know how much I enjoyed it. I thought, "Why not?"

I called the dining room and I got the same woman—I recognized the voice. I identified myself, "This is Lucile Johnson in room so and so, and I just ordered a chef's salad, if you remember, and the boy has delivered it."

Immediately, the woman was on the defensive. How sad, you see, that we so often are. We expect to be criticized. She said, "Why yes, Mrs. Johnson, is something wrong?"

I said, "Oh no, quite the contrary. I have called to tell you that this is the best chef's salad I have ever had. I am delighted you have made such an effort. I want to thank you."

The woman said, "Mrs. Johnson, listen. I didn't make that salad. The girl who made it is Marcy, and she has had something very sad happen in her family today. She has come to work so discouraged. Would you mind telling her this? You know we work back here in the kitchen, and we never hear anything very nice. All we hear are complaints."

I said, "I'd be delighted to tell her."

When Marcy got on the phone, I shared these feelings with her, and I told her I love people who can do their job and do it so well. Her voice had some emotion in it. She said, "Mrs. Johnson, you don't know what you've done for me today. You have made my day." She added, "Something very sad happened this morning, and I needed this."

Now, that was a service that took me only about three minutes. That's all, and I was grateful I had heeded a prompting. There's nothing more nurturing for self than the service you give that you don't get any money for, or any praise or applause for; just those things you know you did that helped someone. Of course its nice to realize your Heavenly Father knows, as well.

I'm challenging you to think of small ways in which you can reach out and serve that can lift and buoy. I, as a therapist, feel most strongly that our lives are composed of little things. Our days, our experiences, they are the little things that can bring us joy and reflect in our faces.

I challenge you, as you contemplate this third S of service, to use your ingenuity, to use your imagination, and to serve in the small ways that you alone can do.

A young woman told me, on one of the BYU circuits, that her father is known as the traveling missionary. He's well along in years, but he carries, in the back of his car, an extra can of gas, and tools, and some water, and even some graham crackers. When he sees people who are in trouble—for instance, if their car has a flat tire—he stops and helps in a loving way, and does so prayerfully. When the people he has helped want to repay him, he never takes any money. Instead, he hands them a card on which he has had printed, "I am a member of the Church of Jesus Christ of Latter-day Saints, affectionately known as the Mormons. We care, so pass this good deed on."

Service-oriented people, beautiful on the inside, create an essence of goodwill and good vibrations, as they live in this life. From a strictly missionary point of view, I, who am a convert to the church, know we will never make a convert to the church until we have made a friend.

Can you imagine what a tremendous impact for goodwill we could have if we committed to the Lord that service would be a part of our development, and we began to reach out in some small way every day to serve, to give, to nurture, to lift?

As the great Prophet Spencer W. Kimball has said, when you have that inclination, "Do it." Do it before the motivation dissipates.

It's a wonderful thing to receive a note of appreciation. It is a lovely thing to hear words of appreciation. Don't ever suppose or imagine that people who are known, and maybe are seen, on lecture circuits, or in front of the public, hear praises all the time, and do not need to hear from you. There isn't a person who does not appreciate and enjoy being told when the things they have written or spoken have been appreciated. Sit down, write that note. A rose to the living is more sumptuous than a wreath to the dead.

Who would appreciate hearing from you today? Sit down and

write that note or make a telephone call. You will be performing a service, not only for them, but for yourself.

I had a young girl tell me that she was able to come back into the church because of one telephone call. She had lost her way because of some very serious transgressions and had found acceptance only among those outside the faith.

She said, "One day, when I was at the very bottom in the things that I had been doing, and I was so lonely, I found myself on my knees, with my face on the floor, just saying, 'What has happened to me? Where am I?' A telephone call came. It was from somebody in the church I hadn't heard from before that I really didn't know very well. But this woman was calling to let me know she cared, and she knew that at this point in my life I was between a rock and a hard place. She wanted me to know the Lord loved me, that he knew exactly where I was.

"She told me she had been between a rock and a hard place in her life, and she was calling to tell me she understood, and she cared. Then, she gave me her address and telephone number and gave me the invitation to write her or call her, if I would. I'm in the Relief Society presidency today because that sister took that moment to reach out across the miles to let me know she cared."

That is service of the loveliest kind when one thinks less of self and more of what they might do to lessen someone else's burden.

I met a perfectly beautiful woman in California, a famous model. She is a convert to the church, and I'd like to quote to you from a letter she wrote to me. She tells how she attended a top modeling school and learned how to do all of these things, and was now before the public, but she said, "I found, after I had accomplished all of these things, I was left with my inner frailties. It was amazing to find that those were my problems, not my physical appearance at all, and I then had to learn how to properly take care of those things that were wrong on the inside. I began with not being so caught up with myself, but more concerned with how I could give and serve others."

This woman, who was already beautiful by the standards of the world, was now discovering the secrets of real beauty, of beauty within.

A STORY OF TRUE INNER BEAUTY

I would like to tell you a true story about my experience with a truly beautiful woman. It happened when I was seven years of age. We lived in San Fernando Valley, in southern California. I was a funny looking little girl with straight brown hair cut in the Buster Brown style, and none of my features ever quite went together. But something happened to me when I was seven years of age that I have never forgotten.

The community in which I lived had invited a world-famous German soprano, Madame Ernestine Schumann-Heink, to present a concert. And Madame Schumann-Heink accepted the invitation.

As a total surprise to everyone, I was chosen to be the child who, at the conclusion of the concert, was to present her with a huge bouquet of roses, and a short speech of appreciation on behalf of the community. The speech had been prepared by the members of the Chamber of Commerce, and I memorized it carefully. I practiced it continuously, in the bathtub, out of the bathtub, before I went to bed, after breakfast. I knew it as well as I knew my name.

The important night arrived and it was the social event of the year. The community hall was packed, excitement rose high. The lights dimmed, and out came Madame Schumann-Heink, dressed in a long, satin gown with a train, and a tiara in her hair.

Madame Schumann-Heink was nearly six-feet tall. To give you a further visual aid, I read recently where she got stuck at one of her performances trying to go through a stage door, and the stage hand had said, "Madame Schumann-Heink, turn sideways."

"Ach, you silly boy, I have no sideways," she said. That gives you a little idea of her size.

This majestic queen began to sing, and I had never heard such a voice in all my life. It nearly took the roof off with its power and majesty! As I watched and listened to this person, who seemed to have come from another world, I was in awe.

At the conclusion of this concert, the audience roared its approval of her performance, and now, it was my turn. The roses had been placed in my hands, and I walked rather unsteadily up the steps and onto the stage. She smiled at me expectantly, but, as I approached her, I froze in stage fright. I could not move or speak, and the awful silence that followed was humiliating to me.

The audience, my mother, everyone was full of such anxiety and it came forth to me wave after wave. Madame Schumann-Heink took a step toward me. "Kinder, you have brought me roses?" I nodded dumbly, and she held out her arms to receive the roses and said, "I love roses." I gave them to her.

Then, in total despair, unable to recall a single word of my speech, I began to cry silently, and tears splashed down my face. I stood rooted to the spot. She looked at me, and then she placed the roses on the stage, dropped to her knees, and stretching out her arms said to me, "Kinder, comen." I walked numbly into her arms. She brushed back my straight hair and the tears from my eyes and said, "Kinder, I love you."

With that a sob escaped my dry throat, and I buried my face in her cleavage, which was considerable, and which held the microphone. Then, for all of those many hundreds of people to hear, I sobbed, "Oh, Madame Schumann-Heink, you are so wonderful! And I love you, too." She held me tightly, rocked just a wee bit as she held me, and the audience for just a second was deathly quiet. But, then, it burst forth in a roar of applause and feeling. They were paying tribute, not to a woman's great voice, but, to a great woman, whose heart was even larger than her voice.

That was over sixty-five years ago but that night I drew a conclusion: all truly beautiful people express their greatness by the size of their hearts. They are kind, they share not only their greatness, they share their feelings. They are beautiful within.

GOD'S MEASUREMENTS

Who is the most beautiful person you've ever met? How the world equates beauty and greatness is different than how God equates it. In the eyes of the world there are constant comparisons. Comparisons in rank, status, strength, power, intellect, wealth, looks, education, culture, skill and achievement. These are all areas in which people strive to excel as a means of attaining greatness. These are ways the world measures personal value.

People are continually motivated to move up the ladder because the world evaluates them in terms of their skills and accomplishments. This places people in a position of competing with one another in a kind of endless striving. As a result, society is structured much like a pyramid. At the top there are a few, select and privileged, who are regarded as genuinely important, truly great, or truly beautiful. In contrast to this handful, there are huge multitudes who feel insignificant in comparison to the great and beautiful ones. They look at what the great and beautiful ones have. They live like kings and queens, they own what kings and queens own, they do what kings and queens do and go where kings and queens go. The great ones have people oooh and aaah over them.

But these are not necessarily the most beautiful people. The greatest people, when measured with God's measurements, need certain qualities.

William Jennings Bryan said that the human measure of life is income. The divine measure is outgo, it's overflow, it's contribution to the welfare of all.

Most likely, you will never sing as a Madame Schumann-Heink, or be a famous ballerina, or a concert pianist, but perhaps more importantly than the fame that comes to such an artist is the joy and satisfaction that can be ours if we develop an appreciation and sensitivity for the feelings of others, and thus be worthy of the divine measurement of outgo.

A friend who had recently buried her mother and was in deep depression came to me for counseling. One day she brought me a poem she confided expressed exactly how she felt. The poem was titled, "My Mother's Diary" and it went something like this: "A few short lines were all she wrote. My mother's ways were simple ones. The day she planted columbines or the day she visited the sick. But one short line from others seems to stand, 'I went to the Post Office,' she would say. I see this one short line my mother wrote from day to day to day. Dear God on high, can mother see tonight these tears I shed for letters that I failed to write."

Who are the people in your life today that you owe a word of love and praise? Your parents? Your grandparents? A teacher? A friend? Be quick to express the positive, to praise. Speak that word, write that note. Do it! Then, you will not need to have regrets. And remember: beautiful actions always contribute to inner beauty.

STROKES OF KINDNESS

I call it the day I had a stroke. The day it happened there was a great deal of stress in my life. Things were beginning to pile up. I was far behind in my work, and this day, which needed to go just right, started out poorly, and it got worse.

Four telephone calls had torn up my morning schedule, then when I was running errands, the back tire went flat. I had told my husband earlier that I was suspicious of it, so it was all his fault! (It is always comforting to have someone to blame.)

In the afternoon, I had two salesmen come to my door. How did they get into the condominium, anyway? Then a call for money, "Mrs. Johnson, we know you have sympathy for the handicapped, don't you?" "Yes, I do," I said between clenched teeth, "because I am one right now!"

I was really getting into my own pity party. "How have I gotten myself into this mess, with all these things to do? At my age I should have peace and quiet and time to myself!" I muttered.

I was primed for the stroke to happen, but I had no warning nor any idea it was on its way. The phone rang, and then, it happened!

The caller said, "Lucile, I don't believe I've told you how much I love you, and how blessed we feel to have had you in our family for over half a century. We so appreciate all you do for all of us." The voice of my precious sister-in-law broke as she said, "I just felt I needed to tell you."

There it was—a stroke. A stroke of love and appreciation and encouragement, right when I needed it! The whole feeling tone of my day was changed.

Let us reach out and touch someone with a call, a note or a visit. You do not know how it might change their day.

How you feel about a person is the way that person makes you feel. Feelings are more important than facts, and others will feel you are beautiful if you make them feel good about themselves.

A CREDIT TO HIS RACE

On a circuit for Brigham Young University Education Weeks one year, I found myself in Houston, Texas, in July. The hotel room seemed sweltering, and I asked the maid just finishing my room if something could be done about my air-conditioner. She said the repair man was out in the hall, and she'd go and get him. A handsome, young, black man appeared. I told him I was a lecturer, and I was so tired and hot I was almost ill. Was there something wrong with my air conditioner? Was there something he could do?

He walked swiftly over to it and with a screwdriver, zip, zip, zip he had the front of it off and said, "Here's your trouble. Your filter pads. I can replace them for you."

I was so impressed with his knowledge, and by his kindly manner that I told him so, telling him honestly that if someone had given me a hundred dollar bill I wouldn't have known what to do to fix that air conditioner. I concluded with these words, "Knowledge is really power. I just so admire people who know their jobs."

He smiled in an appreciative way and then he said, "You know what I'm going to do? I'm going to get you a new air conditioner."

I asked, "Can you do that?"

"Yup. I'm the foreman and the warehouse is right out here in back and it's easy to do. I'll just go get a dolly, I'll take this one out and bring you a new one fast as can be."

In a matter of minutes I had the most refreshing, most vitalizing, refrigerated air you can imagine, and I was overjoyed. I asked the man if he was married, and he said yes. I pressed a bill into his hands and said, "Will you take your wife to dinner with regards from Lucile Johnson?"

He looked at that bill and then quietly he said, "Mrs. Johnson, it's not that I couldn't use the money, but I'm not going to take it. It pleasures me to do something for you that you could not do for yourself."

I replied, "Young man, you are indeed a credit to your race."

He stiffened a bit and he said, "What race is that, Ma'am?"

I quickly replied, "The human race." He smiled broadly and extended his hand. "Mrs. Johnson, I'm glad we belong to the same race."

And I said, "Son, so am I."

WE GET WHAT WE GIVE

We do not give to get, but the law of life sees that we usually get what we give. One evening, at Hotel Utah, I addressed the Young Homemakers of America where they presented me with a beautiful red, white, and blue corsage. My husband attended this function with me, and we stayed overnight in Hotel Utah.

The next morning, as I was in a hurry to leave, I saw my corsage of the night before fresh and lovely as ever, and we decided it would go perfectly with the blue suit I was wearing. I put it on, and as I rushed out of the door, a maid, who was about to knock, almost fell over when I opened the door so suddenly. I said, "Ooo, I'm sorry. I didn't mean to knock you down. Are you the maid?"

She was as old as I, her hair was bleached and badly so, and a tooth was gone from the front of her mouth. Her shoulders sagged, and her face looked despondent and defeated. I asked the maid, "Isn't this a hard job for you?"

She nodded and said, "It's the hardest. When I go home at night, my arms and back ache so I cry."

"Can't you get another job?" I asked her.

"No. I'm untrained, I'm uneducated, and this is all I can do; and I have to work. My husband is an invalid and I have a teenager still at home."

I said simply but honestly to her, "Well, you do a good job. The rooms here are absolutely, beautifully clean."

She smiled a little sadly and said, "Thank you. You know, we maids never hear anything like that."

Then, on an impulse, I took off my corsage and I said, "Tonight, when you go home, I want you to tell your husband and teenager that you were voted the best maid in Hotel Utah and were given this corsage to prove it." I smiled as I pinned it on her uniform, but I was totally unprepared for her response. She put a work-worn hand to that corsage, and then she burst into tears.

"I will keep this corsage forever. It is the first one I have ever had. Could I just give you a little hug?" I said I would be flattered, and there we stood in the hall of Hotel Utah, she crying softly, and my eyes also wet. As she pulled away, she said to me, "You have made my day." And I replied, "And you have made mine."

Have you ever imagined there are those who grow old and die who have never had a corsage in all their lives? A rose to the living is more sumptuous than a wreath to the dead.

One time a little girl came running to her mother with a soft, blue feather in her hand. "What bird dropped this feather?" she asked.

Her mother said, "I don't know the exact bird, but I can tell you the kind of bird it was. It was a bluebird."

Everywhere we go in life, we leave a feather. People may not know exactly who we are, but they always know the *kind* of a person we are. Feelings are often more important than facts, and beauty is in the eyes of the beholder.

If you would be beautiful within, be very careful of the critical and the unkind word. As a university student I wanted so badly to be accepted by a particular sorority I had pledged. My senior sorority sisters had the pledge sisters brought slowly in front of them and turn carefully so we could be properly judged. I was wearing a shoe that is popular today. It is a shoe with the toe and the heel out. It's called a sling heel. At the conclusion of my trial by my peers, I was told, for my own good, of course, "Lucile, don't ever wear a sling-heel shoe. There seems to be something wrong with your heels, and when you walk, you walk like a duck."

That has been over fifty years ago, and every time I go to a shoe clerk I hear myself say, "Don't show me an open-heel shoe. There's something wrong with my heels and when I walk, I walk like a duck." My married daughters have assured me that my heels aren't any different than anybody else's heels, but you see, we have memories like elephants for the critical word, the labels we have heard.

TWO LITTLE WORDS

At the end of one of my programs I had a man come up to me and say, "Sister Johnson, I want you to give me one sentence, only one sentence that can help me in my marriage. Don't give me a whole sermon, because I don't want a sermon, I want a sentence."

I said, "I can do better than that. I can give it to you in two words."

He asked, "What are they?"

I replied, "The words are these, 'Be Kind.'"

Those words also summarize the way to be beautiful within. Every day you will meet somebody who is hurting or smarting who needs encouragement, who needs to be treated with kindness and not ignorance or impatience.

When we do for others who cannot do for themselves, we are blessed in special ways, for this is Christlike service. Christ did for us what we could not do for ourselves.

When we care for the handicapped or crippled, this is obvious Christlike service. But those who nurture, lift, listen to, and buoy up others, are also doing for others what they cannot do for themselves and, thus, they, too, become like Christ.

Kindness *will* make a marriage successful, but when you apply the advice to "be kind" to how you treat yourself and how you treat every person with whom you come in contact, you will be beautiful.

Everyone has the power to become beautiful if not already so. Everyone also has the power to help others become beautiful. Use the power, and it will change your life.

⇜ 9 ⇝
To Thine Own Spirit Self, Be True

....

I AM A CHILD OF GOD

While my husband was in Viet Nam, I was associated part time with a university in Texas, where I was living. One evening, I was invited to join some ministers, chaplains, and other faculty to address a group of people who had been invited for a free smorgasbord dinner. The only fee they had to pay was to listen to the speakers. At the conclusion of my speech, a large man approached me. He was very unkempt, his hair was messy, he wasn't clean-shaven, and his clothes were rather disreputable. He made a very deliberate walk toward me and said, "Mrs. Johnson, I want to talk to you, and I want to talk to you right now!"

I must have drawn away just a little, because he said, "Listen, Ma'am, I'm tough."

I didn't doubt that, and I didn't want to have an altercation there, so I said, "I'll be happy to talk to you."

Of course, I was lying through my teeth, but I asked, "Where would you like to talk?" He motioned to an area, lifted me up by the elbow, and we moved into that area. I'm going to edit his language somewhat, because it was very colorful, but let me tell you what he said to me.

He said, "Mrs. Johnson, I'm an orphan, and I've never married. I really have no friends. There isn't anybody who gives a tinkers d— whether I live or die. But," he said, "something happened to me today, and I don't have a single soul to share this with, and after I heard you speak I thought maybe you'd listen to me."

I was convicted by my conscience, and I said sincerely, "Sir, I have a hundred years to hear what you have to say. Let's sit down here."

He began, "I'm a bus driver in this lousy town, and there is no job in the world that's lousier than being a bus driver. People gripe at me and nitpick. They are on my back all day long. Today it was so hot, the wind and the sand blew, and people complained, pushed, and shoved. I suffered all day long. It was the end of my run. I'd let my last passenger off nearly three blocks back. Now was going to be the happiest time of my day. I was going into the closest tavern and spend the rest of the night cooling my parched throat. Then I looked up into my rear view mirror, and I saw a black woman and her two kids sitting in the back of my bus."

He said, "Something just popped inside of me and I was so furious. I turned around to her and said, 'What in the blankety-blank-blank are you doing sitting in this bus? Don't you know you were supposed to get off three blocks back? Now get off this bus!"

He said, "Those little kids got up and ran down that aisle, and jumped off, but not their mother. She sauntered down that aisle until she got to where I was, and then she put a hand over my hand—the one that was holding the door open so she could leave, and I could hardly move. Then, she moved close to me and put her face right up to mine, and this is what she said.

"She said, 'Mr. Bus Driver, I'm very sorry we didn't get off where we were supposed to, but we're strangers in El Paso and we didn't know where to get off. Before my children and I go back to the motel, I must tell you something. I have enjoyed this ride, and I thank you for it. But I know that deep down inside where you live, you're hurting, and crying, and bleeding. The reason I know this is because I have hurt, and cried, and bled so much myself. But do you know, Mr. Bus Driver, something has happened to me that has given me hope. Do you know who I am, Mr. Bus Driver?'"

The bus driver said to me, "Of course, I didn't know who she was. I really didn't know what she meant. Then she said, 'I'll tell you who I am. I am a child of God and so are you. And when my children and I get back there to our motel, we are going to pray to our Heavenly Father that some day you can come to know that you are a child of God, too.'"

He said, "Mrs. Johnson, I looked up at her. There were tears in her eyes—tears for me—and they splashed down her cheeks. She smiled at me, then turned and got off my bus."

He concluded with these words, "Now Mrs. Johnson, I want to ask you something. I don't know this woman; I'll never recognize her again if I ever see her, but there was something that happened to me. Something . . . I don't know what. I sat there, and I couldn't move. I just sat there and watched her as she took those two little kids and walked down that dusty path, and then let me tell you the other thing that happened. They began to sing a little song with those same words in it. Now, I'm no musician, I don't know much about music, but I will remember this song because it said, 'I am a child of God and he has sent me here.'

"Mrs. Johnson, I want a true answer out of you. I want you to tell it to me like it is. Is it possible that one person—just one person—maybe somebody you'd never seen before, can say something that gives you a little hope, that kind of screws your head on right?"

And I said, "Mr. Bus Driver, you'd better believe it's possible! You *are* a child of God. That's what it's all about. When you understand what that means then life takes on meaning. You understand you have a Heavenly Father who knows exactly where you are and he loves you. You begin to understand that all experiences, good and bad, have purpose." And then I shared with him these wondrous lines from an unknown poet. They go like this, "I saw him once. He spoke a word that laid my spirit bare, then passed beyond my ken. But what I was I will never be again."

In this life we look out for each other one-on-one. You row your brother's boat across the swells, and lo, your own has reached the shore. A familiar song says it poetically: "No man is an island, no man stands alone. Each man's joy is joy to me, each man's grief is my own." Edward Everett Hale said it another way: "I am only one but I am one. I can't do everything, but I can do something. And what I can do, by the grace of God, let me do."

OUR FIRST ESTATE

When I was introduced to the Church of Jesus Christ of Latter-day Saints, the principle of our pre-earth existence, the first estate, became the most awesomely beautiful concept I could imagine.

The concept that you and I did not have our beginnings as some biological entity here on earth, but rather that we came from a magnificent celestial home on high, where we were begotten by and claimed by our father, none less than God, and were born to a beautiful celestial mother, who is the queen of heaven, is so stunning in its magnitude, that even after all these years, I am overwhelmed with the beauty of it. We all had a most auspicious beginning, as that bus driver was just beginning to learn.

In that pre-earth life from which you and I have come, we grew from spiritual infancy to spiritual maturity. I believe the covenants that are now a part of our lives, our acquaintances, and the loving relationships we currently enjoy all had their beginning there.

Our education in that pre-mortal life must have been expansive. I believe our training experience was detailed and complete, that we were not flung forth to come to this mortal probation without training. How provocative to think, as we grew from spiritual infants to spiritually mature persons (and I don't know how long that took), that we rubbed shoulders with the great and noble ones.

How often did you and I sit together, side by side, to be taught great and enduring principles, so that during our mortal probation we would be able to find our way back to that eternal home?

I am sure in our pre-mortal home we knew something of the pain we might experience in our second estate. Yet, you and I shouted for joy, the scriptures tell us, when we contemplated coming here to earth and taking on the mortal body that had been prepared for us.

When Father proposed his plan (for the plan of salvation *is* our Father's), it was our elder brother, Jesus, who stepped forth and said to our Father, "Send me." We thrilled at his willingness to sacrifice himself to save us from death and from our sins and carry out that plan for our eternal benefit.

We knew the years here would be short, but they would be important. I am sure our education included instructions on how to keep our first estate, and that if we did keep it, we would have the opportunity to keep our second estate and thus be added upon. You and I kept, in a very real and wonderful way, that first estate. We have earned the right to be here.

When we came forth to this sphere of mortality, a tiny mortal body had been prepared for us by our mortal parents into which this spirit personage, which is our real self, could come and have a mortal home.

When our spirits enter this mortal body, we do not remember who we are or where we came from. That is part of the plan and part of the test. However, the gospel of Jesus Christ helps us remember who we are and who we can become.

Unfortunately, too much of the time, we do not see ourselves as Father would have us see ourselves. We see ourselves as the world sees us, or as Satan sees us, and we become discouraged. Brigham Young said one day that if he could bless the Saints, he would give them eyes to see things as they really are. If I could give you a gift, so that in some remarkable way you could see with your spiritual eyes, you would be able to discern who you really are.

If you could see your real self, your spirit self, you would see a person so beautiful or handsome, so brilliant and capable, so loving, kind, and obedient, that in your awe, your inclination would be to kneel. You would say, "Am I that awesomely wonderful person?" I could assure you indeed, that is exactly who you are.

William Shakespeare penned some words you and I are inclined to quote often: "To thine own self be true, and as the day follows night thou canst not then be false to any man." As I've contemplated that great truth, I've wondered if we know to which self we should be true. I think we need to put a greater emphasis on the self that too often we're not even aware of—the real spiritual self to whom we must be true.

In our mortal life, it is extremely helpful to remember that it is not our mortal body which gives us worth, it is that great spirit body, that great spiritual entity which we are, that brings us worth, and that worth is eternal.

You and I might represent many differing nationalities and inherited traits. However, the color of our skin, the nose we have inherited, or the color of our hair and eyes really isn't important when we consider to whom we all trace our genealogy.

YOU HAVE SUCH WORTH

Our youngest son, Gary, and his wife, Lori, came over to visit us for a few days while we were on our mission in London. We bought tickets for *Phantom of the Opera*. Because the tickets are expensive and hard to get, we wanted to make sure we were there on time so we wouldn't get locked out.

On our way to the opera, we took the subway and then walked from the subway to the escalators. There are many unsavory looking people in those areas. Generally, the scenario is that you look neither to the right nor left, you just get on that escalator.

As we were moving along, an old tramp of a woman came up to us. She looked almost inhuman—hair matted and grey, a dirty face wrinkled and creased, and a hand like a claw. She had layers and layers of dirty clothing and newspapers over her body. As we started for the elevator, she grabbed our son Gary by the arm. She said with a snarl, "Give me money for a smoke, sonny."

Gary stopped, looked at her, reached into his pocket, and got out a couple of pounds. As he put the money in that old claw of a hand he said, "Don't spend this on a smoke, get yourself some food. Get yourself some soup, something that would be good for you."

"Oh, sonny, what does it matter what I spend this money on? I'm just a worthless old tramp."

Our tender boy said to her, "Don't you ever say that about yourself again. You are not worthless. You have great value."

A good number of the British people had stopped for this encounter and heard these words. Then, in that moment, it seemed a metamorphosis took place. That old, wrinkled, dirty face softened, and that claw of a hand somehow had a more tender womanliness about it. She said, "Young man, thank you for this money, but more than that, thank you for those words. In my whole life I have never been told I had any value."

How many old tramps or bag ladies do you have in your neighborhood? Probably not very many. But there are people who, though they wear expensive apparel, feel inside that they have no worth. When I tell this story, people often say to me, "Sister Johnson, I know how that tramp lady feels, because that's exactly how I feel."

Be very careful not to listen to voices in your mind that would have you be discouraged and dismayed, that tell you that you do not measure up, or that tell you that you can't succeed. Don't believe it, because those are voices from the dark side. Remember who you are and that divinity flows in your veins. We all trace our genealogy to God the Father, the author of it all, and to a beautiful, magnificent, celestial mother. You have such worth. And what our eternal parents want for us is to return to live with them one day. To help us fulfill this plan for our lives, the Lord answers prayers in his own way and in his own time and gives us guidance all along the way.

OUR DIVINE INDIVIDUALIZED
EDUCATIONAL PLAN

For those in the field of education, the initials IEP are significant. They stand for Individualized Educational Plan. In our school system, there are people who have special needs. As a result, individualized educational plans have been developed for many of them. Generally, a person in the field of special education, together with the parent and the student, works out the kind of special plan needed.

I believe that our Father in Heaven has on file, in some celestial office, a divine individualized educational plan for each of us. We each have different needs and Father knows that. But in Father's planning, there is really only one goal for all of us, and that goal is that we will one day return to live with him. Our individualized educational plan provides the experiences we need to help us return to him.

Elder Neal Maxwell, speaking to this topic, said, "The Lord will customize the curriculum for each of us in order to teach us the things we most need to know. He will set before us in life what we need, not always what we want or what we'd like."

President George Q. Cannon said, "God has chosen us out of this world and has given us a great mission. I do not entertain a doubt myself that we were selected and foreordained for our individual mission before the world was, and that we had our part allotted to us in this mortal state of existence as our Savior had his assigned to him." Yes, our individual mission on earth is a part of our divine IEP.

The most serious threat to fulfilling our mission is the conflict that goes on within ourselves. We are composed of a duality, our spirit self and our mortal self, sometimes referred to by psychologists as the negative self. Descriptive words such as carnal and devilish cause us to wince, but they are true descriptions, and this duality precipitates the conflict.

Our spirit self and our mortal, carnal, negative self have been joined for our divine education. When the choice was made by our first mortal parents to partake of that forbidden fruit, certain things happened just as Father had said. He told them the veil of innocence would be removed from their eyes, and it was, and he told them they would be subject to death, and they were. But they were also given increased agency. We have come to this earth school with lessons to learn and tests to pass or fail, according to the choices we make. If we fail, we will be called to repeat the class until we learn the lessons that are here for us to learn, but we always have a choice.

God is not content with us as we are today because he understands fully our potential and what we can become. He knows of our divine IEP and he is anxious for us to fulfill it so that we can return to be with him.

"MY BROTHER WAS VERY SAD"

My husband and I were in Atlanta on a Sunday where the Primary provided the service. As a part of the Primary program, a beautiful little black boy spoke about his brother. His family were converts and his brother had gone on a mission. He said, "The place my brother wanted to go on a mission to was Africa, and he had prayed to go to Africa. But when he got his mission call, he went to California, and my brother was very sad."

Then the little boy held up a picture filled with people—beautiful people in tribal dress—and he said, "When my brother was on his mission in California, he converted a man, a black man, who was a prince in his country. When that prince returned to Africa after he was baptized, he baptized his entire tribe, and he has sent this picture to us."

Could that young man from Atlanta ever have imagined, when he prayed to go to Africa, that Heavenly Father had a divine IEP for him that was to be executed in a different way than he expected? It was to be executed in the way our Father determined. Heavenly Father answers prayers. He may not answer them instantaneously, but from my long years of experience with prayers having been answered—though some are answered only after an apparent delay—I want you to know they are answered. But they are answered in our Father's way and they are answered in his time to fit our IEP.

THE ROLE OF OTHERS IN OUR IEP

I want to introduce you to a family whose name is Hernandez. They moved from Venezuela to London. Dr. Hernandez was a medical doctor studying to become a neurosurgeon. Proselyting missionaries in our London mission knocked on their door and gained entrance, and we subsequently became involved with that family. It was an immediate adoption. We loved this family so much. But as we worked with them, and as their understanding of the gospel and the Church began to grow, they began to get telephone calls from family members in Venezuela saying to them, "Beware. You are becoming involved in a satanic cult."

Arlena was close to her mother, and her mother would call and weep and say, "I am going to die. I'm going to die if you go forth with your plans to join the Mormon church, and your father is going to have a heart attack."

One day Sergio called me, and he said, "Sister Johnson, we love you. You are our other parents, but we must ask you and the missionaries to no longer teach us. Though we want you in our home, we cannot have one word of the Church mentioned because Arlena is about to have a nervous breakdown."

That baptism was put on hold. I was devastated. I had known this family for less than six weeks and, yet, these people meant so much to me that I paced the floor at night wringing my hands. "Oh Lord, please. I know this family has the believing blood. I know that they are supposed to be baptized. What can we do? What can we do?"

What I did not know was that Heavenly Father had an individualized educational plan already in operation for the Hernandez family. In my minuscule ability to comprehend God's plan, of course, I didn't really understand how things could work out. But this is what happened.

I want you to meet another couple whose name is Seranos. They come from Chile. They are converts to the Church, and he had been on a mission. Spanish is their native language. They came to London because she was a high school teacher, and he was a neuropathic doctor, and they wanted to get some advanced education. However, they came to London unprepared for the variance between the sterling pound and their monies from Chile. Very quickly they were without money.

The one place they knew to call was the visitor's center in Hyde Park. The day they planned to come to see us, they discovered they didn't even have enough money for a subway ride or for a double-decker bus. They hadn't had enough money to even have breakfast that morning.

That wonderful young couple knelt and pled with the Lord. This brother said, "I think we could use just three pounds—that's all we need—three pounds. That will get us to the visitor's center." In north London, on that busy thoroughfare, hundreds, and maybe thousands, of people that morning had passed by. But, as they walked like two children holding hands, with their heads down, they saw a soft drink can, mashed by many feet, in front of Sergio Seranos' foot. He kicked that tin can and under it was exactly three pounds!

Father's IEP for the Hernandezes and for the Seranoses began to advance. I wish I could tell you I had so much spiritual understanding that when they arrived at the visitor's center I thought, "Hallelujah! This is the family that Heavenly Father is providing to help the Hernandezes." That wasn't the case, but the Seranos family needed a place to stay. Arlena and Sergio lived in a flat under quite primitive conditions, but there was a small room that, I thought as I called Arlena, maybe the Serranos family could rent, because I knew the Hernandezes could use the money.

I wish I could tell you it was with deliberation I didn't tell them they weren't to mention the Church, but it just slipped my mind. When

Brother and Sister Serranos knocked on their door, the Hernandezes were prepared to say, "We are sorry," but Arlena said, "We instantly knew that they were to be with us."

That night as they sat on the sofa, the Church began to be discussed, and for every protest that Arlena would make, Gabriella would say, "That's exactly the way it was with me. My family disowned me. Of course, now my family are all in the Church."

At 2:00 a.m., telephone calls began to come from Venezuela. Isn't it interesting how the dark forces move in at the most strategic moment? But who was there to diffuse these calls? Brother and Sister Seranos.

With the Seranoses' help, and with the background that had already been given, all the Hernandezes' doubts and misgivings were overcome. Brother Johnson and I were there a few weeks later to watch that family go down into the waters of baptism.

The Seranos family was there all the time to help the Hernandezes become educated spiritually for their temple experience. Brother Johnson and I were given leave that day to be with them. We had fasted as we went into the temple with this family, and it was, perhaps, the most awesomely beautiful experience we have ever had.

The Hernandez family is now living in Venezuela where Brother Hernandez is a practicing neurosurgeon as well as a bishop. All of those people in Venezuela who made calls to warn the family about the "satanic cult" are now members of Bishop Hernandez's ward.

Where are you at this point in your life? If your life does not have the most desirable circumstances, perhaps you are wondering, "Why me?" or "Why now?" Could these circumstances be part of your IEP? Remember, each of our lesson plans have to be different, but our goals are exactly the same—to return to live with Father.

Let me tell you now about a family that comes from Provo, Utah. A mother and a father with a temple marriage were divorced after thirty-five years. The heartbroken family of grown children just couldn't believe it. But these were the mother's words, "I have suffered indifference from your father, and emotional and mental cruelty. I have had thirty-five years of his selfishness. He thinks only of his own needs, he complains, he even belittles me, and I can't stay in this marriage any longer. It is not a celestial marriage, and I've got to get out."

After the divorce, she put in her papers to go on a mission, and she told me an interesting thing about her mission call. As a senior sister, she was assigned to another senior sister for the whole eighteen months of that mission! That doesn't happen very often. In fact, it is almost unheard of.

After eight or nine months, one of the daughters began to receive letters from her mother saying that her mother was miserable. She had a sister companion who was a disaster, who was absolutely driving her up the wall. Her letters were full of woe and anger. "Please go to somebody," the mother begged.

The daughter went to the bishop, then to the stake president, and then to the missionary committee, who said, "The mission president is the one who has to be contacted. He's the only one who can make a change. That is the chain of command."

The mission president was contacted, and he prayed about it and said to this good woman, "I'm sorry, but I can't change your companion. This is the companion the Lord wants you to have and I'm not to separate you."

The mother and daughter were crushed when no companion change came about, and the sad letters continued to be sent home, but more and more in these letters were the words, "This sister companion is so much like your father I can't believe it." Every complaint she had ever leveled against her former marital companion she was now leveling against this sister. But before her mission was over, she started establishing her priorities. She knew she had to learn to live with this sister companion in love, patience, and forgiveness. Of course, she did not realize that was a part of her individual educational plan from her Heavenly Father.

After eighteen months, she had learned she could live with her companion. She had learned to not only live with her but to love her in spite of her failings and her frailties. When that woman came back from her eighteen-month mission, and I met her, she said to me, "I learned to love and appreciate my sister companion, but that experience gave me the ability and the tools to live with my husband again, to love him more, and even to appreciate him as my eternal companion." That was a part of her IEP.

What is your IEP? Perhaps, you are where you are because it is a part of the divine educational program that Heavenly Father has for you. Heavenly Father knows things about us we do not know. Inevitably, we need to come to grips with those things in our divine IEP that are essential.

ESSENTIAL ELEMENTS OF INFORMATION

In the military, EEI stands for Essential Elements of Information. Data is gathered from various sources and includes where the enemy is located, how well-fortified they are, and what their numbers are. With this assembled data, generals then make decisions that affect thousands of lives and even the outcome of battles. The most serious consideration in the assembly of all known data is its accuracy.

In order to return to our Father's celestial home, we need accurate EEI. Accurate and essential are the key words in that phrase. In our personal lives there are three categories of information: nice to know, important to know, and essential to know. Essential information is any information that will help us return home safely to our Heavenly Father. We receive accurate essential information from the scriptures, from the current prophets, and from personal revelation to us as we pray for help and guidance.

However, it would seem logical in our divine IEP that our Heavenly Father would also have provided EEI for us to make our return journey home. Among the many essential elements of information we are taught in the scriptures are three principles that I believe are of paramount importance. Regardless of our age or stage in life, I believe that these three principles will always be primary factors in our development. In other words, we never outgrow them. They are the principles of obedience, forgiveness, and love.

OBEDIENCE

Everything we do should have one purpose, and that is to bring us to Christ and help us to obtain the goal of returning to live with Him and our Heavenly Father. Obedience is the essential element in this goal.

A story from my own family illustrates obedience. It is fun for me, as I go throughout the world, to meet relatives of mine whom I didn't even know about who have joined the Church. One of these is a cousin I met in Idaho who was young enough to be my son. He told me his conversion story.

He had gone to a Christian college in Idaho where they met together in a communal dining room for the night meal. The chancellor of the college called him to say grace, and he was totally unprepared for that because he had not experienced saying grace in his home. He said, "I couldn't think of a single grace except one Dad used to say around a campfire, and so I said, 'Good food, good meat, good Lord let's eat!'

"My friends all thought that was really funny, but the chancellor didn't think it was funny, and he expelled me from college. I didn't think that was very Christian.

"When I got home, I got a call within a few days from an old high school friend, and he asked if I would go with him to have something to eat and see a movie. Then he said, 'Oh, by the way, this won't mean anything to you, but I am a stake missionary in my church, and I have a lesson to teach to a family, but my companion can't go with me. Will you be my companion?'"

Loren said, "The only thing I heard was 'steak,' and that sounded good, so I said okay. When we got to that farm home, it wasn't long before I was caught up in the spirit of what my friend was saying. I'd never thought of him as particularly brilliant, but all of a sudden I was aware of his tremendous knowledge and the spirit with which he imparted that knowledge to this farm family."

Then, my young cousin said, "I felt some stirrings in my heart that night I had never experienced before, and when he let me off in front of my dad's house, I walked into the granary. I remember there was a beautiful harvest moon. As ignorant as I was, I dropped on my knees and offered a prayer pleading with Heavenly Father that if there was one bit of truth in what I had heard tonight, and if he would confirm this for me, I would promise to be obedient, and I would do whatever he wanted me to do, whether I wanted to do it or not."

My cousin went on to say that he called his friend the next day, was taught the lessons, and was baptized. Subsequently, he went to the University of Idaho at Moscow. The first Sunday he was there, the bishop spoke in a powerful way about the fast. He said the next Sunday was fast Sunday, and though it would seem difficult, and a great disciplining factor, he pleaded with them to have a meaningful fast that week and to understand that the fast was not a principle of sacrifice but a feast for their spirits.

He continued, "The following Sunday when I came back to church, the Bishop invited me to administer the Sacrament. When I began to read the Sacrament prayer, the words began to blur, and I fell forward in a dead faint with my face in the Sacrament tray."

I asked, "Loren, what happened?"

He said, "When I heard that bishop talk about the fast, and what a sacrifice it would be, I thought he meant we were to fast from that Sunday to the next."

I said, "Loren, you mean you fasted for an entire week and didn't have anything to eat?"

He said, "I drank water, but I didn't have a single bit of food, not even a crust of bread."

When I asked him how he could do that, he replied, "I thought I would die. I even dreamed of bread, but each time my hand reached out for a piece of bread, I would remember a harvest moon and my dad's granary when I asked our Father if he would let me know for certain that the Church was true. He had let me know in no uncertain way because when I got up off my knees in that granary there was such a burning in my bosom, I knew there had to be some physical evidence. When I ran up to my room and pulled up my shirt, the upper part of my torso was as red as if I had been in the noonday sun. Our Father had let me know for certain, and I had promised him obedience, and that is the reason I was able to fast for that length of time."

Most of us do not have such a dramatic opportunity to be obedient. But obedience, whether in minuscule ways or very large ways, is an important part of our training that makes it possible for us to return to the presence of our wonderful Heavenly Father and celestial mother.

One of our great high councilmen, Brother Watanabe, is a Japanese man. He told me he was born in Sendai and his father was the first convert in that city. He said, "My father was a man who had the greatest love for the gospel of Jesus Christ. In a very unoriental way he insisted on sharing the good news with any and all that he could get to listen. He carried several copies of the Book of Mormon around with him to give to anyone he could get to accept one. This is very unlike the Japanese personality."

Brother Watanabe said, "As a teenager I was embarrassed about my father. I remember one day in particular. My father and I got on a train in Sendai for another town, and my father put me in between himself and a man sitting next to the window. During that entire train ride, my father insisted upon speaking to this man about the gospel of Jesus Christ and the restoration. The man was humiliated. I was humiliated. I thought, 'What have I ever done to have a father like this?' When that man got up, my father shoved a Book of Mormon at him.

"Later, I went off to school at Brigham Young University. Then, I got my mission call. Do you know where my mission call was? Was it to some land that my oriental language background would help me? No, not at all. It was to Brazil—the furthest point away from Japan you can find.

"I knew there had been a mistake in Salt Lake City. I said to my father, 'You have to call the mission committee. Surely they wouldn't want this boy that can barely speak English to have to learn another language out in Brazil!'

"My father asked me one question, 'Do you love the Lord?'

"With my own father asking me a question like that, I had to say, 'Yes, Father I love the Lord.'

"Then, he said, 'If you love the Lord there will be no problem with this mission call. You will go forth and do what the Lord wants you to do, and that is in Brazil.'"

Brother Watanabe said that when he arrived in Brazil, he immediately joined a group of missionaries teaching English lessons to a little group of Japanese people who had recently moved to Brazil. A father and mother and their three children were taking the English lessons, and their thirteen-year-old girl was very intrigued with what the missionaries really were there for, and asked many penetrating questions. The missionaries were careful about their responses so as not to jeopardize the opportunity to teach the English classes, but she entreated her father to let them come to their home to tell them more, and the father said that it would be all right if they came to teach the family the gospel of Jesus Christ, and they very soon set a date for baptism.

He said, "Here I was a junior companion, a greenie elder, and we had a family ready to go into the waters of baptism. My senior companion was elated. But the night when they came for the baptism, the father said to us that he was very sorry, but he had changed his mind. He thought his decision had been premature. He wasn't ready to be baptized. But he said his daughter could be baptized, with his permission, because she would be brokenhearted if he did not allow her to go ahead with her baptism."

Brother Watanabe said, "I heard myself say something that horrified my companion and even startled me. I said 'We cannot baptize your daughter.' The man wanted to know why, and I heard myself telling him about the home from which I had come. I told him, 'I had a father who loved the gospel, who honored his priesthood. I could have been a disobedient teenager, but I was raised by a father who was always obedient to the Lord. Where would I have been today if I had not had that kind of father? I cannot possibly think it would be right for your daughter to be baptized and grow up in a home where there is no priesthood and where the gospel is not lived. I do not think that is fair to your little girl.'

"The man looked at me very strangely, and then asked, 'Where in Japan do you come from?' I told him Sendai. The Japanese father then asked, 'Do you have a picture of your father?' I said I did and he said, 'Let me see it.'"

When Brother Watanabe showed this good Japanese man a picture of his father, the man began to cry and he said, "I know this man. He is a man who, on a train in Sendai some years ago, embarrassed me as he insisted upon talking, preaching about a gospel of Jesus Christ restored. As I got up, in humiliation, to get away from him, he thrust a Book of Mormon into my hand, but I dropped it in a trash can. Now, all these years later, half way around the world, the Lord has sent this man's son to give me a second chance and to teach me the gospel of Jesus Christ."

That family went down into the waters of baptism in obedience to the truths they were taught.

FORGIVENESS

Forgiveness is a powerful principle that is absolutely essential to our eternal progression. On our journey back to our Heavenly Father, lack of forgiveness can be like a great roadblock to our progress. Pain of such magnitude comes from our inability to forgive! I would say that lack of forgiveness is one characteristic universally present in unhappiness and despair.

I have a friend who is a convert to the Church whose husband became romantically involved with the woman who was responsible for my friend's conversion. It was really a sad chain of events. The woman who had been the missionary and my friend's husband ran off together, abandoning two families. You can imagine the repercussions in that ward, that stake, and those families. A long, bitter time passed, but then the two came back and went through the hard process of repentance and a church court proceeding. Their respective mates were both willing to take them back.

My friend, who I will call Louise, who had taken her husband back, said to me one day, "Lucile, my ex-friend, who ran off with my husband, called me and asked if she could come to speak with me, and I thought, 'Yes, you come because I want you to hear some things. You have no idea what you have done to me. You have done such harm to me.' I wanted her to hear those ugly words from my own mouth because they had nothing to do with the church court, only with my feelings.

"When she knocked on my door, I opened it, not to that attractive, rather sensuous-looking woman I'd always known, but to someone who looked like a young animal who was terribly afraid. She came in and sat on my sofa, and I sat on the other end. She said, with tear-filled eyes, 'Louise, you must forgive me, because, if you don't, I cannot survive.'"

Louise continued, "I had a spiritual experience, at that moment, in that situation, because the Lord, somehow, allowed me to feel what my friend was feeling, almost as though I were inside of her, so that her thoughts, and everything about her, were mine. Her agony and remorse were so terrible, and I felt the tumult of her soul so intensely that it was as if her flesh were dying. I knew, in that split second, that the Lord Jesus Christ, by his grace, had offered me a chance to experience, in a minute way, some of the things he experienced in Gethsemane. He, so innocent, had willingly experienced them. I ran to my friend, and we dropped to our knees in front of that sofa, embraced, and shed tears. Healing began for both of us. And now, Lucile, I am free from hate and anger. At last, I am free."

Forgiving is the only way to be fair to ourselves because getting even is a loser's game. Unforgiveness leaves us with more pain than we received in the first place. It's a hook that hurts each time we think about the person who wronged us. The only way to heal the pain is to forgive the person who hurt us. Forgiving them stops the rerun of pain and releases us from the hook so that healing can take place. It is like cutting a malignant tumor out of our lives. No one can make us forgive, but for-giving *is* freedom.

Fred Babble, the author of many fine books, was our gospel doctrine teacher when we lived in Washington, D.C. Fred told us a story about a man who had been sent home from the hospital to die. Doctors could find nothing physically wrong with him, but his body processes were ceasing. Brother Babble and another brother from the Church went to his home, and Brother Babble said, "I was giving this man a blessing, and I was stunned at the words I heard myself say. The man looked like he was dead already. His face was grey and his breathing shallow.

"But I said the words the spirit had me speak. I told this good brother the reason he was dying was that he was so full of hate and anger and ugly unforgiveness his body could no longer function. I then reminded him of the great atoning sacrifice of the Lord Jesus Christ who has made it possible for the beautiful gift of repentance, and if he, by the grace and love of the Lord Jesus Christ, could understand what he had done, and would move through that repentance process, I promised him there would come a day when he would rise from his bed and go forth to fulfill the measure of his creation."

The man opened his eyes, a tear rolled down his cheek, and he asked Brother Babble to please help him turn over because he wanted to show him his back. Brother Babble said, "I've never seen such a back. It was layered with scar tissue. He had obviously suffered tremendous beatings. I said to him, 'Who did this to you?' He replied weakly, 'My loving father.'

"He then told about a father who was a drunken sadist, who had beaten him so badly that sometimes, as a little boy, his underwear would run red with blood. He said, 'As soon as I was old enough to escape that home and the brutalizing of my father, and what he had done to both my body and soul, I left. And you're right about being unforgiving. There isn't a night I haven't pled with the Lord to wreak some horrible vengeance on this father for what he had done to me. But, I have heard you speak by the power of the Spirit, and I know I have sinned in those angry feelings. If you will help me, I will do the things I must do to repent.'"

The story moves on to a dramatic conclusion because that man was eventually strong and well, and he went to another state where his elderly father was living. As he walked in front of that little frame house, an elderly man was sitting in a rocking chair on the porch. He walked up those steps, now a man in his prime. He stood before a father who at first didn't recognize him, but when he did, he cowered back in his chair, recognizing a son who he was sure had come to take his life.

Instead, that strong son dropped to his knees before his father, buried his face in his own hands, and in tears said, "Father, I have come here to beg your forgiveness. I have sinned against you so mightily. All my life I have prayed and pleaded with Heavenly Father to bring retribution to you. I have sinned, and I cannot live another day with peace until you will grant me forgiveness."

The old man, weeping and shaking, said to his son as he embraced him, "I was an evil and sick man, but I have never drawn a free breath since you left our home because I feared you would come to take my life. You would have been justified, but instead you're here begging my forgiveness." He said, "You cannot know what this means to me. It is as if a black and heavy cloud has been taken from my soul."

Two men, after many years, and through the power, the atonement, and the love of the Lord Jesus Christ, felt the bitterness and hatred dissipated from their bodies.

The prophet Joseph Smith said,

Nothing is so much calculated to lead people to forsake sin as to take them by the hand, and watch over them with tenderness. When persons manifest the least kindness and love to me, O what power it has over my mind. (Joseph Smith, *Teachings of the Prophet Joseph Smith*, sel. Joseph Fielding Smith [Salt Lake City: Deseret Book, 1938], 240)

I work with members of the Church who have been abused or molested—very often by members of their own families. These people must themselves have Christlike qualities to survive such cruel and inhuman treatment. They have a supreme test and an opportunity to become saviors on Mount Zion for those sick family members who are spiritually and emotionally disturbed and who have consequently abused them.

Forgiveness is a principle that brings peace into our souls. We must learn to forgive if we would be true to our spirit self and free to continue our journey back to our Heavenly Father.

LOVE

There is only one power that is sufficient to allow us to forgive completely, and that power is the healing force and power of love. Love is not a weak and fuzzy-wuzzy thing. Love forgives because love is the most powerful force in the world. Love is the ultimate, creative, healing force and power.

Love is the force that made it possible for you and me, who have a divine heritage, to be born into that first estate as spiritual infants. It is the power that caused the universe to be created, and the power that the Lord Jesus Christ manifested as he bled from every pore in the Garden of Gethsemane and bled again on Golgotha.

The Lord Jesus Christ took all his teachings from the Old Testament and combined them into two commandments. They have to do with the power that comes from love. The commandments are to love the Lord with all our might, mind and strength and to love our neighbors as ourselves.

The kind of love Christ referred to is more than a feeling. We are talking about love, the verb, which requires action. That kind of love surely means to care so much about another that whether or not it is convenient or timely, or whether or not we have the energy or desire, we will walk with, reach out to, put our arm around, speak to, and listen to those who need us.

This kind of love is sometimes scary as we reach out and risk ourselves because sometimes we will be rebuffed. As we attempt to do kindly, loving things, people may look at us like we have crawled out from underneath a rock somewhere. But that really doesn't matter. We covenanted when we were foreordained that we would minister to each other—and what that means is to love each other. Our spirit self requires the commitment and consecration of the kind of love Jesus exemplified. The Lord Jesus Christ, our elder brother, will make it possible for us to employ that kind of love, if we make ourselves worthy and ask.

"HE NEEDED SOMEBODY"

An elderly man was dying in a military hospital. He had been asking for his son. A young marine finally came into the hospital, and the nurse came to get him. She said, "I'm so glad you've come. Your father has been waiting for you."

The young marine looked perplexed, but followed the nurse to the bedside of an aged man who was very close to death. When the nurse said, "Your son has come." The old man lifted up a feeble hand and a smile came to his face. That young marine grabbed the feeble hand and sat down by the man's bed and stayed there holding that hand, murmuring soft words to the dying man.

The nurse was not able to convince him to leave for a single respite. In the wee hours of the morning, the old man died. When the nurse came to make the arrangements, the marine asked a puzzling question, "Who was that old man?"

The nurse said, "What do you mean, who was that old man? He was your father."

The marine said, "No, he wasn't. I've never seen him before in my life."

The nurse was flustered and said, "Well, why didn't you say something?"

The marine replied, "I didn't protest because I could see how badly that old man needed his son, and his son wasn't here. He needed somebody, and it was my role to be that somebody."

Showing love and kindness may not always be convenient—generally loving someone is going to cost us something—but our spirit self is nourished when we give love and kindness, when we reach out to minister and to help.

GIFTS OF LOVE

We have a daughter who is a single parent with three children. She has two jobs to help meet their needs. As often as possible, on the weekends, we are with her and the children to give all the help and support we can for this precious family. One Saturday, I arrived at her house early to help with the housecleaning, washing, and all the endless tasks that mothers and grandmothers are so familiar with.

It was strawberry time, and we had a case of strawberries to make into jam in addition to all the regular tasks. I told Ashley Ann, who was twelve, that I needed to do some grocery shopping but that we would make strawberry jam together when I returned if she would prepare the strawberries while I was gone. My instructions were, "Wash the berries carefully, and take off the stems."

When I returned to the previously clean house, bedlam reigned everywhere! Only a small bowl of smashed strawberries were visible, and the children had been joined by our other grandchildren, making a total of six who had been making Kool-Aid and sharing popsicles, graham crackers, and peanut butter. The kitchen was a shambles.

I asked, "What happened to the rest of the strawberries?" Ashley Ann, in tears, said, "Grandma, it's very hard to take the *skin* off a strawberry!"

"The skins?" I squawked. "Oh no, not the skins, Ashley Ann, the stems!" That is when I lost my cool. Placing six grandchildren in front of me, I lectured them about making such a mess and told them the "evil of their ways."

David, who was seven, said, "Grandma, you aren't supposed to talk like that."

"Why?" I asked.

He replied, "Only mothers talk like that."

My response was not kind. I said in loud tones, "Well, too bad! This is the way this grandmother talks, because this is the *real* grandmother, and this is the way this real grandmother feels."

Ashley Ann stepped into the hushed circle of wide-eyed grandchildren and said, "This is not the *real you* grandmother. You are tired and exhausted, and you need to take a nap!"

The tension was broken as I admitted, almost tearfully, that I was very tired, indeed. All six children happily took up the task to help poor, tired Grandma. They took me to the sofa, and each grandchild hurried to provide a gift of love.

One child got a wet cloth for my head. It was not wrung out sufficiently and it dripped into my ears and down my face. One child provided his very own popsicle and popped it into my reluctant mouth. One child got a brush and attempted to "do" my hair.

Another child kissed my hands and face, while another child rubbed my feet. All of them were so tender and concerned, all of them giving small tokens of love and affection.

When one asked softly, "Grandmother, are you feeling better?"

I took the popsicle out of my mouth, asked for a towel to dry my face, and then I told them I felt much, much better. "But Grandma, why are you crying now?"

"Because I love all of you so much and in so many ways I can't even count them."

That day those precious children helped me to remember my true, loving self. They nourished me spiritually with love in a way I will never forget and helped me get back to a frame of mind where I could, again, begin nourishing them.

To our eternal, spiritual, real self let us be true. And let us make sure that our eternal self is nourished by performing acts of love and kindness to others and by reflection, prayer, and meditation. To become more aware of nourishing our spirit self is one of our primary responsibilities.

We have no problem remembering to nourish this mortal body. Under any circumstances, we make sure to feed our mortal bodies. But we need to be aware of the nourishment our spirits need so that we can create a strong and healthy spirit self. Our spirit self, our real self, yearns for the right kind of nourishment to keep him or her strong, weeps when we err, would have us love, forgive, be ministers, and magnify the calling to which we were ordained in that great pre-earth experience.

That eternal self to whom we have covenanted to be true knows the things that are necessary for us to do in this short probationary period of mortality, such as obeying, forgiving, and loving. Some of the things we need to do will be difficult and will stretch our abilities, but we can do them with the help of the Lord.

IS ANYTHING TOO HARD FOR THE LORD?

There is a scripture that became very meaningful to me as Elder Johnson and I served a two-year mission in London. It comes from the thirty-second chapter of Jeremiah. We became aware of what a powerful missionary Jeremiah was, and whenever we thought things were really heavy and hard on our mission, all we would have to do was read about Jeremiah, because he had one of the toughest missionary journeys you can imagine, all of his life.

We read in that chapter where the Lord is calling him, it would seem, to another missionary assignment, and Jeremiah is lamenting. Then we hear our Savior say, "I am the Lord, the God of all flesh: is there any thing too hard for me?" (Jer. 32:27). Why do I share this with you? I want us to contemplate that thought. Is there anything too hard for the Lord? There absolutely is not.

Some missionaries we were acquainted with in London were called to a rather questionable area to teach the gospel. They drove up to a flat and noticed some rather rough-looking characters loitering about. It was with some apprehension that they locked up their car and went into the flat. When they came back out, the tough looking-characters were still there. They ran toward their car, opened the doors, jumped in, slammed and locked the doors, and tried to start the car. It would not start. While one missionary was working to get that car to start, the other one was praying with every fiber of his being, asking the Lord to please deliver them from this.

Suddenly, wham! The engine started and off they roared. The missionary who had been praying looked back and saw that the thugs were all standing out in the middle of the street, open-mouthed, watching their car leave, as if they were greatly surprised.

When they got far enough away from that dangerous area that they felt safe, they pulled their car over to the side of the road and turned off the engine while they had a prayer to give thanks to God for delivering them safely out of that dangerous situation. Then they tried to start the car again, and the engine wouldn't start. They were in no great danger now, so they got out, lifted up the hood, and looked in, and then they discovered why the car wouldn't start at first—it didn't have a battery! The thugs had cut the wires and lifted the battery out. No wonder they looked surprised and amazed when this car started!

Is anything too hard for the Lord? As we are true to that eternal spirit self and seek to live the truths we knew in our first estate, I hope we will remember that we each have our Individual Educational Plan, that the Lord has provided the Essential Elements of Information we need to fulfill our plan, and that he will be our partner in fulfilling the plan.

During the hard times, remember what the Lord said to a discouraged Jeremiah, "I am the Lord, the God of all flesh. Is there any thing too hard for me?" He who can cause a car to start without a battery can help you to live up to your divine potential, help you fulfill your IEP, and help you be true to your spirit self.

~~ About the Author ~~

Lucile Short Johnson grew up in California with an insatiable interest in other people. She has always loved to hear people's stories, problems, fears, and victories. She lives and breathes these varied experiences, and they have each become part of her. In this book, Lucile shares some of her favorite stories and the wealth of knowledge she has gained from these experiences.

Lucile is a talented, natural-born speaker, but that is not her greatest talent. She is also a gifted listener who shares every feeling, every hurt and joy anyone is able to express to her, whether face to face, on the telephone, or in a letter. Listeners know that Lucile hears with her heart, discerns the unseen tears, the humor inherent in a situation, and the growth that has taken place.

While Lucile was attending college, she met her husband and then joined the church. Lucile is the mother of five grown children and the wife of Colonel H. O. Johnson, who had a long and distinguished career in the U.S. Military. Lucile faced the challenges of frequent moves and heavy responsibility because her husband was away so much.

Learning has always been important to Lucile, so she continued taking college classes by correspondence. She went back to school for advanced degrees when she was a grandmother. She began speaking and counselling extensively when her children had largely grown.

Lucile says she is a marriage counselor, and not a divorce counselor.

She encourages her clients to keep a "glad" book, not a "mad" book, to look for rainbows they hadn't noticed, to know that life is a training ground for imperfect people, and to realize that our growth is what counts more than anything else.

Lucile says that marriage involves two imperfect people and that the real joy of marriage comes from the growth we experience as we handle the problems and challenges together over the years. Her own marriage of over fifty years, which has weathered the storms of many separations and great personality differences, exemplifies all she teaches in this book. She seems to be one who really does practice what she preaches.

Among the best loved women speakers in the Church, Lucile has addressed thousands of people over the years—the majority of them women—and has touched their lives and their hearts. She knows adversity well, and has experienced her fair share, but believes whole-heartedly in learning from it and looking on the bright side. This is essentially the philosophy she shares in this "sunny-side-up" book.

ARLENE BASCOM has been preparing for the opportunity to bring Lucile Johnson's exceptional words of wisdom into print for many years. She helped create and edit *Latter-day Woman* magazine and has done a great deal of freelance writing and editing.

Arlene feels this book is the most exciting of any she has worked on. She has always enjoyed Lucile Johnson's tapes and Education Week classes, from which this book was created. Arlene and her husband, Gary, have seven grown children and fifteen grandchildren.